AUTOBIOGRAPHY OF
LORENZO PETTY, SR.
EDITED BY F. BLOUNT

Deadly - Gangsta "1" is the autobiography
of Lorenzo Petty, Sr.

Second Edition

Owner and author Lorenzo Petty, Sr.
Printed in the U.S.A. By Publishing Concepts, LLC
Cover Art by Lorenzo Petty and F. Blount
Graphic Design and Layout by Terry Tomlinson
Photos by Lorenzo Petty Family

ISBN 13: 978-1-933635-48-4
BIO002010 BIOGRAPHY & AUTOBIOGRAPHY
Cultural, Ethnic & Regional / African American & Black
1 2 3 4 5 6 7 8 9 10

DEADLY - GANGSTA "1"

Deadly - Gangsta "1" is the autobiography of Lorenzo Petty, Sr. Mr. Petty proclaimed by law enforcement and the news media as one of the deadliest gangsters that prowled the streets of St. Louis during the 1970's.

Mr. Petty grew up during a time in St. Louis when racism, hate, poverty, degradation, hopelessness, and crime were woven into the landscape of black ghettos. He was nurtured in a sub-culture where immoral, decadent, and illegal behaviors were endemic. Lorenzo's youth was one dictated by his conditions. He decided early in life on how he would survive; he would employ the Rules of the Jungle and demand respect. He resorted to criminal behaviors in order to survive and obtain material possessions. He was driven by a force that was uncommon among his peers in the world of crime. He displayed a mental capacity that was rare, and a ruthlessness that was unequal in his world.

He became King of the Jungle.

Lorenzo's life was not unlike that of the multitude of most young black males' who were trapped in a bottomless pit, becoming involved in criminal behaviors for various reasons. However, Mr. Petty was driven by a force that was unequal in the criminal and killing business. At an early age he became involved in criminal and other debilitating behaviors, as well as becoming locked into the criminal justice system.

This work will document the lives and actions of the Petty family, as told by Lorenzo. In this autobiography, Lorenzo relates in vivid details the lives of the Petty Boys, their mother, and their family. The Petty family stood out in their neighborhood – their lives dictated by race, geography, and circumstances.

5

Editor's Note

The image that has been portrayed of the Petty family, one of criminal endeavors and the brutality connected to it, has been distorted by the news media. Observing and experiencing from a distance affords a more enlightened, unadulterated, and positive view of the Petty family.

Those who have had the opportunity to witness the exploits of this unique family tell a story other than the one painted by law enforcement and the news media. Many people have come to over-look the feared and gangster reputation of the Petty brothers; those with the understanding and capacity, for forgiveness.

Lo, as he is called by those close to him, possessed a capacity to endure what life brought his way. He has possessed the essence of humankind: faith. He has truly been blessed. His survival and will power will serve as fuel for countless young black men in America who are in need of someone like Lo, who has been blessed. His legacy will be one of survival and his faith in God!

"My family arrived in St. Louis in 1946 or '47", Lorenzo says. From their union, they had four children. My sister, Annie Ruth Petty, passed away when she about two months old. My brothers and I were born at Homer G. Phillips Hospital, which was located on the North Side of the City. Back then, if you were black and poor, your babies would be born at Homer G. (which is what it was called) or you would be brought to City #1, which was located on the South Side of the City. Homer G. Phillips became known as a hospital that specialized in treating gunshot wounds, cuttings, and stabbings. The black-only doctor staff saved many black men who had been involved in violent encounters from which they were not expected to survive.

In the criminal world when someone got shot up, and didn't die, the first thing that the shooter asked was "Which hospital did they take him to?" Someone would say "Homer G." The shooter would say "He's going to make it." Homer G. had that type of reputation. So if you were a true killer you had to be about your work, or constantly be lookin' over your shoulder, or end up in in prison or in the bone yard; none of these options were good.

The first elementary school we went to was the neighbor-hood Curtis Elementary School. Our house was about two blocks from Curtis. Back in those days, we did not have any lunchroom at Curtis. Sometimes we would go home for lunch. Mama would have some lunch meat or hot dogs and pork 'n' beans. There were many days we did not have anything to eat. Sam knew how to write like my mother and he would write out a note for food, sign my mother's name and take it to the grocery store. Sam got so good at it that he started signing the back of my mother's checks for her and cashing them. Sam was always real smart. Matter of fact, he was the smartest one among my brothers.

We went to Curtis Elementary School from the ages of five to ten. At that time we played around in our neighborhood, which was mainly in the 2800 block of Sheridan. That's where the Cody family lived. Mr. and Mrs. Cody had about twenty-four children, more boys than girls. They were the largest family that I knew of on the North Side. We were like brothers and sisters because we lived and grew up in the same neighborhood. Back in those days we all came up like one big family. We were able to eat at their house and they were able to eat at our house. When we cooked, we put on big meals, because we knew who was coming over. We made sure we had enough because at most of our meals all three of us ate at least two plates of food. Sometimes I would eat three plates, if Mama let me. She would make me be the last one to eat, at least until Sam and Joe had ate. Since I was the one that ate the most, Mama made me wash the dishes all the time, and clean the kitchen up. She even made me cut the wood for our stove. I was the one who got up every morning to make the fire for the stove. Sam and Joe acted like they were unable to make the fire right. But I had my way of getting back at them. At night when I got up to piss in our bucket, I acted like I missed the bucket and pissed in their shoes. When they woke up the next morning their shoes would be wet.

Our house was a small four-room house. In the winter time we all slept in one room, which was the room that had the stove in it. We all would get into one bed, during the winter. This bed had three or four blankets on it. My brothers and I wore them one piece long john underwear, with the booty part opening. Plus, Mama was a big woman, weighing about three hundred and seventy-five pounds. Her body gave off a lot of heat, especially behind her booty. That was my favorite spot, until I decided to piss back there. Sam or Joe would roll in it and their draws would get wet. I would get up and let my draws dry out before morning and put them back on. Mama would beat whoever's draws was wet. They would always cry and say "Mama, it was not me, it was Baba Bro" (which is what they called me.)

During the winter Mama had to get us ready for school. Man! It was so cold out there and the wind would blow so hard until it would freeze your face. Mama would put some pork grease on our faces to keep "em from freezin." Our ears and noses felt like they were going to fall off. Also, the tears that were falling from our eyes would freeze on our faces. We were too poor to buy gloves, so Mama made us put socks on our hands to keep them warm. We had very little clothes that were in good enough shape to wear to school, so, we had certain clothes that we wore only to school. When we came home, we had to hang our school clothes up, and get back in our old clothes. Sometimes in the summer we ran around the neighborhood with no shoes at all. Man! Our feet were so tough so that when we stepped on a rock or piece of glass, it didn't even hurt. But we had them old red-brick sidewalks, and every now and then, I would kick one of the bricks that was sticking up and hurt my big toe. Our shoes were in such bad condition that they had holes worn through the bottom of them. We had to put newspaper in our shoes to help protect our feet. Mama could not afford to buy shoes often, being on welfare. We had Sam's Shoe Store in our neighborhood. Sam was a Jew who wore thick glasses and the store's shoes were real cheap. The shoes that everyone was wearing back then were Chuck Taylor tennis shoes. If you had a pair of them you were real cool! Every time we got new shoes we went outside to race each other. We thought the new shoes had something to do with how fast you were able to run.

Many times we were hungry and all we had was some welfare food. Welfare food like powdered eggs, powdered milk, lunchmeat, cheese, peanut butter, oatmeal, cornmeal, flour, lard, and butter. From these foods and other items we were able to make some very tasty meals. Back in them days there were a few black families that had money; but with those that did, I was cool with their children. Whenever I got hungry, they took me to their house and I ate like it was my house.

I had become a strong enforcer in my neighborhood. With my fightin' skills and warrior tactics, respect for me grew. I was a person you didn't want to run into, if it could be avoided. Most of my friends were cool people, but they did not have that killer instinct, and they needed it to survive in the ghetto. No man wanted to be disrespected and have his manhood belittled every time he went somewhere, especially in front of his woman. I was the enforcer in my family. It became known, if you had problems with one of my brothers, I was the one you had to watch out for. If one of us had a problem, we all had one and would use any force necessary to win.

My mother was a cold woman and she was not scared of anyone; she would fight real quick. She would whip us, if we came home crying about what someone had done to us. We would then get another ass whippin'. My brothers and I were like shepherds in our neighborhood over those who were weak. We would not let anyone come to our neighborhood and mess over nobody. We had lots of people in St. Louis who considered themselves to be a part of our family because whenever they told a bully they were one of our relatives, the bullies would leave them alone. Our family had a reputation for comin' and handlin' their business. So now I see how God used us because my family made a difference in the lives of many in St. Louis.

We went through a lot in our lives. Back in 1962 there was a dance place called Melvin's located on Jefferson and North Market. Everybody from downtown went there—it was the place to be. There also was Dance Land located on Vandeventer. There were lots of fights at Dance Land; somebody got their ass whipped there every night. Melvin's had some fights but not that many, not until Bow started coming around who started robbing people for their clothes.

One day Bow ran up on my brother Sam and tried to rob him for his coat. Bow jumped Sam, but Sam got away, ran home and got the .22 rifle that Mama kept at home for protection. Sam put the rifle under his topcoat and went back to Melvin's place. When Sam got to North Market, Bow came out of Melvin's with some more people. Then Sam started shooting at Bow. Somebody said "Bow, they are shooting at you." Then Bow jumped on top of a car and said "You can't kill me." Sam then fired about three or four more shots at him. Then Bow fell off the car to the ground. Someone then hollered, "Bow, get up! Bow get up!" They then hollered out, "Bow is dead!"

Sam was the first one of my brothers to go to prison for killing someone. He was fourteen years old at the time. They

Deadly - Gangsta "1"

sent him to Boonville, an institution for boys. I was thirteen years of age at the time. My mother took me and Joe to see Sam a couple of times.

Right after that, I had been hangin' out in the Pruitt-Igoe housing projects. I started goin' to Pruitt-Igoe around 1960. By 1963 I had met a lot of people in the Projects. By this time my brothers had been transferred from Curtis Elementary School to Duvall Elementary. We met new friends and some of our cousins, who we had never known before. Their names were Clarence and Charles Star. I also met another big brother. His name was Ronald Philippor.

Duvall was located on Dayton Street at Glasgow. Gamble Community Center was right behind the school. We all were going to Duvall School around 1960. Just like we had control of our old neighborhood around Cass and Leffingwell, we took control of this neighborhood. We were the Petty family and we had the Cody family behind us. That was a strong force.

When we joined forces with the Star family and Ronald Philippor, we were runnin' Duvall School. At that time they had a lunchroom. Lunch at school was about thirty or fifty cent. But there was a little store right across the street from Duvall. They sold chili, hot dogs, and hamburgers. They were about a dime. Man! If you had thirty or forty cent, you could buy a nice meal. Everybody that was with us did not need any money. Because we would walk around outside the store and get money from the children we knew that had money. We would ask for nickels and dimes until we had enough to buy a meal. We would do this every lunchtime because we were poor and their parents had money and they always gave them extra.

I did not like school because I could not read or write that good and I was too embarrassed to let the children at school know. I wanted to be hip and grown up. I was too worried about what someone had to say about me that was negative. Also, I was a very slow learner and people in those days did not want to take that much time with you. So I did not go to school that much. I was in the streets hustling. At that time they had a juvenile officer, who was out in the streets durin'

11

school hours, lookin' for children who were out runnin' the streets during school hours. When I found that out I started hanging in the Projects with my Project family. I started to really like hanging out in the Projects because the police did not mess with you, like they did whenever they saw you on the streets. Whenever we did see the police in the Projects, we would run up in the buildings and they knew they were not going to catch us. There was about fifteen or twenty of us that would go hustling every day together. We would hustle up and down Jefferson, Franklin, and Cass Avenues. We would be lookin' for trucks that would be carryin' chickens, eggs, whiskey, or anything we could sell. Anything that we got we would turn in the Projects. Because then we would sell it for little or nothing. All we wanted was enough money to get high and buy something to eat. There were several places in the neighborhood that sold cheap eats. There was a Bar-B-Q place on Jefferson, London and Sons on Jefferson and Cass, and a Chinaman's place on Jefferson and Franklin. High Wheels was at Elliot and Madison—they had the best tripe in St. Louis. Plus, up on Franklin, there were all kinds of places to eat. You could take a dollar and buy a nice meal. Once we had made a hustle and got full, we went to the 905 store located on Jefferson and Dayton. Across the street from the 905 was a pickle company and down the street was another Bar-B-Q place.

Man! We'd buy some white port, put a pack of Kool-Aid in it, and prepare what we called a Shake 'em Up. We then would buy some weed and get messed up! We would then go to the Projects, and look for a dance under or in one of the buildings. Man, them cats in the Projects could really dance, especially the cats with us. Frank Banks was the best dancer among us, and Big Boy was the next best. There was a dance place called Bubble on 19th and Coleman Street. It was close to Carr Square Village. We were taking a chance when we went down there. But every time we went down there, there was about fifteen or twenty of us and would be messed up off that white port. That shit would make you fight anybody. The next day you would be sore as hell, eyes all black. And your head would have hills on it. The first thing you would say, "Man, I'm not going to drink no more of that white port." But the next day you would be drinking some more.

We would not buy the wine because we were too young. We would catch some ol' wine-head outside the liquor store and he would cop for us. They would never put the wine in our hands. They would put it on the ground and walk away. Mantia's Liquor Store was right around the corner from Bubble's dance place. It was a popular place where lots of people would hang out.

Man! We use to hang out up and down Franklin. Startin' shit with people and robbin' drunks. Sometimes, when we were around the liquor store, we would take peoples' liquor bags from them. And run to the Projects and get drunk. We knew they could not catch us because we all were young and could run.

Well, Duvall Elementary kicked me out and sent me to Pruitt Elementary. They put me in the Special Room. I had been in the Special Room at Duvall but I was used to being there and I knew everybody very well. In the Projects I had everybody thinkin' I was 18 or 19 years old. When they saw me in Pruitt, they were asking "Hey Lorenzo, what are you doing in here?" I would say, just visitin' y'all. I did not come back to Pruitt School.

At that point in my life, I was wild. One day we took lots of chickens and eggs off a truck. The owner of the truck ran after us but everybody got away. About fifteen minutes later he (the truck owner) ran up on me and said "Where is my shit?" He tried to arrest me and I hit him three or four times in the face and ran off in the Projects. Later on he came up on me in a police car. He told the police "Here he is" and they arrested me for armed robbery and assault. They sent me to Missouri Hills, a young boys' institution. When a person was sentenced to Mo Hills you could be there until the people at the institution thought you had made enough progress that you could return home. In other words, if you was messing up, they could keep you there as long as they wanted to. At least until you turned twenty-one. I was sent there in about February 1964 and I was housed in Cottage 5. Our house parents who ran the cottage were married. We cut down trees with a cross saw, and cut grass with a push mower. Man! That grass cuttin' shit was hot in the summer time, and that cutting down trees was hard work. Plus the husband wanted me to do all the cutting with the cross saw because I was a big guy. I had to think of a way out of this. Well, I found out that his wife needed someone to help clean the cottage. I told her that I knew how to clean and fold clothes, so she hired me. I turned out to be what she was looking for. Her husband got mad because he wanted to know why she had to pick the biggest guy. She told him I was the only one who really knew how to clean and fold clothes the correct way. Man, I was so happy about that because when I finished working, House Mother made me a very nice sandwich and gave me a cold drink; I also got to be in the air.

Around 1964 my brother Sam came home from Boonville and I got a furlough from Mo Hills. We got a chance to run around the neighborhood with my brother Joe. We ended up at Curtis School yard on Madison Street. There was a lot of action going on in the schoolyard; drinkin' and gamblin'. Someone told me about these pills that everybody was getting high off of. I asked, "Where do I get some?" They pointed out this dude and I walked up to him and told him I wanted to buy some. He told me that he did not know me and to get out of his face. I knocked him out, took all the pills and passed them out to anyone in the schoolyard that I knew. Man, everyone was so high and it wasn't until I had to leave that I found out I had overdid it. I didn't know them pills were so strong. My system was real clean because I had not had any drugs in a long time. Joe and some of my friends saw my condition and took me home, which was only a few blocks. Once we made it home, Mama wanted to know what was wrong with me. They told her I had drank too much; this was in 1964. I kept trying to go outside, but my friends wouldn't let me. I then started to get upset and violent. I started fighting those who were attempting to hold me back. They let me go and my brother Sam grabbed me. Then we started to wrestle; I was still trying to get loose

14

to go back outside. Mama thought we fightin'. She then went to the kitchen and passed out, while Sam was still holding me. Then someone called 911 to send a doctor, because they thought Mama had had a heart attack. Besides sending a doctor, they sent the police. Now I was in the middle bedroom with Joe holdin' me. Sam went to see about Mama.

The police entered the living room and asked where the heart attack patient was. I heard someone tell them she was in the kitchen. When they walked toward the kitchen they walked up on me and Joe, who was still holdin' me. They asked Joe what was wrong with me and Joe responded, "She's in the kitchen". Then I responded, "There isn't anything wrong with us, mo" Then one of the officers drew back his nightstick to hit me, but I hit him first. We started fighting the police and ran them out the house. Everybody else that was in there ran out the house too. I ran to the back porch. Something told me, man, you started this shit, you can't leave them.

At this time Sam was about 16 years old, I was about 15 and Joe was 14. When I went back in the house, the living room was full of police. A police attempted to hit me with his nightstick, but I beat him to the punch. The police were beating the shit out of Sam and Joe. They both had about five officers on both of them. They were just about to overtake both of my brothers, until I jumped in and started to help. I freed Joe first and then I freed Sam. They both ran out the house and the police then started beating my ass. They brought me out the house by my arms and I was attemptin' to break loose. Someone bust me in the back of my head and almost knocked me out. They attempted to throw me up in the police wagon. I was trying to avoid getting thrown up there. My brothers and friends who were already in the police wagon, pulled me up in there, before they killed me. They locked up a bunch of us.

Many people went to prison that year. It was the year of that riot—the first riot to take place in the history of St. Louis, Missouri. Everybody who got locked up in that riot got broke up and busted up. They had to take us to the hospital. My head was busted up and Sam's arm was broke. We were all held in the Ninth District Police Station. After they arrested us there was about twenty or thirty of us in one cell. Everybody went to sleep. I woke first and looked around at everybody; they were all busted and broke up. I laughed at everybody because of the way they were messed up. Then someone said, you must not have looked at yourself. I looked in the mirror. My face was busted up. I then started to feel a lot of pain everywhere, in my head, my face, arms, and back. Man! Everywhere was hurtin' on me. Matter of fact, that mornin' everybody started to feel the pain. Later I felt somethin' in my pocket. It was the pills I had took from the dope dealer. They were downers and would help with our pain. They had not gotten us treatment for our injuries or pain at the hospital. Man, I was passin' out pills to everybody that was in the cell and we were gettin' high all over again.

They came to get us out of the cell, getting ready to transfer all of us to different jails because of the different ages. Some of them went to City Jail; my brother Joe and myself went to the Juvenile Detention Center located across the street from the Central District Police Station. They kept the boys on the third floor and the girls on the second floor. The gym was on the fourth floor.

The same day that we got there they had all of us sit lined up together in this room. Then lots of white people came in and started walkin' around the room lookin' at us. Man, I had never seen so many white people at one time in my life. I guess they wanted to see who were these bad guys who had caused all this trouble. Right after that, they started making arrangements for us to go to trial. Sam was sent back to Boonville for the second time. They sent me back to Mo Hills. Joe was committed along with me. It was his first time being committed.

At the end of 1964 I ran away from Mo Hills. I was stopped by the police in the area but they were unable to contact Mo Hills. They couldn't hold me long since they didn't have a reason. I had told them I was eighteen. They asked me what I was doing out there. I told them I was riding with this dude and his ol' lady when they started fighting. She jumped out the car and I jumped out to get her. When she got back in the car, they drove off, and left me. The police cut me loose and I continued my walk home. When I got home, Mama sent me to Chicago to live with my father's sister Amanda. Aunt Amanda's daughter Jo Ann, got me a job in Chicago. But I didn't like it so I came back to home. I started runnin' around in my ol' neighborhood, hangin' out in the Projects and gettin' high.

At this time I was goin' with a girl name Shirley. Man! Shirley was really cool and she had lots of heart. Everywhere I went Shirley went with me. One night in December of 1964, we went to the Capri Center; it was about twenty or thirty of us from Pruitt-Igoe. They were havin' a dance. Once we got there, we started puttin' some money together to buy some wine and beer. I put 25 cent on it. When they brought it back, I was dancin'. By the time I got there, it was all gone. I asked my friends where was the drinks. They said they drank them up. Then this dude stepped from the crowd and said, I drank it. I turned around to see who said it. It was this dude name Lee, and there were lots more dudes with him. I did not see any of my friends at that time. That's when I became scared. By that time the security guard had come over to where we were. He told Lee to leave me alone. The guard then said "Let's go." When I turned to follow the guard, Lee spinned me around and hit me. I then stabbed him with my knife. I then ran from the area, with Lee and some more dudes with bats chasin' me. I fell down in the dark, and they ran past me. When I got up, I started to run towards the Projects, but the guard pulled a gun on me and I had my knife out. That's when Shirley ran up and jumped in front of me and put her arms around me. The security guard told me to give him my knife; I refused. I told him if he took me back there, they would kill me. I finally gave him the knife. Someone then hollered, "Lee is dead." When the guard turned to look over his shoulder, I broke and ran, and made it to the Projects. I spent a night at a friend's house. The next day I got up and was walkin' home. The police saw me and I ran up in this yard on Leffingwell and Sheridan. I got up on the roof of the barber shop there and laid down. When the police stopped lookin' for me, I got down and went home. I lived in the next block. When I got home, my Mama was there. She had not yet heard the news. I told her what I had did. She said "Lord! What am I going to do? Lord, this boy is going to run me crazy."

Mama ended up callin' Officer Norwood who was a juvenile officer at the Ninth District. She came and got me and turned me over to homicide detectives. Larry Venlimiglia and Herb 'Seek and find' Riley, were the officers who would be the ones that picked me up. They would not ask me many questions, because of my juvenile status and I never had anything to say. They took me to the Ninth District Police Station, where I was jailed. Eventually, they took me to the Juvenile Detention Center. My mother ended up hiring attorney James Bell, because they wanted to certify me and try me as an adult. This did not happen. They ended up sending me to Boonville. They had just sent Sam back there. That meant that we both would be there together. Sam did not like that because I stayed in all kinds of trouble. He knew that if I got into somethin' he would get into it too; that's the way our mother raised us, to stick together. We were a close family when it came to each other.

When I got to Boonville they put me in G House. My work force was the Hunter Force. We did it all—in the winter we shoveled coal from trains. We would shovel twenty tons of coal in the morning and twenty tons in the afternoon. One team would shovel it from the train to the ground and the ground team shoveled it into the power plant. Man! It was winter time but we got so hot until we were working in our tee-shirts. Sometimes we would shovel snow around the compound or go out and cut down trees. In the summer time we would plant things when the time came. Man! Workin' in that hot sun was something else. The last thing we had to do was cut that dry-ass corn down for them cows. Man, that shit got all down in your clothes, and made you itch and scratch like hell.

Anyway, I ended up working in the dairy, milkin' cows, and shovelin' cow shit. We had to get up every mornin' around four and were through milkin' around six or seven. When we finished we would go to the kitchen and they would feed us bacon and eggs for breakfast. We could eat as many eggs as we wanted to. That was the only good thing about working in the dairy. Our boss was a white man and he was real mean. He liked watchin' us fight each other. We had what they called a smoke room, where everybody would sit around and smoke when they were finish working. That's when the boss would make us box each other. He would make me box everybody because I was the biggest and everybody was always talking about how good I was with my hands. After I had whipped everybody's ass, he would make all of them jump me. I would still beat all 'em ass. Man! I was hittin' so hard, nobody wanted to run up against me. The boss hated me. One day I was out back, looking at the bulls. The boss lied and said I was pla-yin' with the bulls, in a sexual way. Then he took me inside to whip me with this big board that he had. I kept telling him that I had not done anything. So now he wanted me to bend over so he could whip me. Man, I had on this thin ass jump suit, with no draws on. The first time he hit me, hurt like hell. He was going to give me five hits without me raisin' up. Every time I raised back up, he would start the count over. Man! I was never good at taking whippings. After he hit me that first time, I was not gettin' down any more. Then he took me into his office and locked the door. When he did that, everybody knew he was goin' try and beat some ass. But I was not scared because I knew he couldn't handle me. He sat me down and told me, let me smack you and it would be all over with. I told him, "Hell no, are you goin' out of your mind?" He then jumped up out of his seat and started hittin' me in the back. He couldn't hit me anywhere else, because I was covered up pretty good. He beat me 'til he got tired. He finally stopped and let me out his office.

I had various run-ins with the guards at Boonville for some reason. They always wanted to beat on you. One time this guard name Weed wanted me to hold my head down in front of him so he could hit me with this shovel handle. I refused to do it. He then tried to hit me anyway but I caught the handle in my hands. He then started yellin' like a wild animal. He kept on trying to hit me and I kept catching the handle. When he saw that I was not going to let him hit me, he took me to the Administration Building to report my conduct to the so-called big boys. Anytime they had and inmate who refused to cooperate, they would take them into the cloakroom, which was located in the Administration Building, and there they would jump on you. When everybody saw them take me into the cloakroom, they knew I was goin' to get my ass kicked. They went and told Sam. He went and rounded up other brothers and they camped outside the Administration Building. They were ready to run in there if they started beating me. They knew I was going to fight back. I think the big boys knew what was going to happen when they saw the brothers gathered outside the Administration Building. Plus they knew we had a reputation for not taking any shit, so they let me go. When I came out the cloakroom, I had tears in my eyes, because my feelings had been trampled on, by the way they were talkin' to me. After it was over Sam asked me if they had done anything to me. I said no. Sam had a razor blade in his pocket. Well, I did not have any more problems from those in charge of the institution.

Sam went home before I did. He came back for the second time in 1964 and went home in1965. I had come to Boonville for the first time in 1964 and was released in 1966.

While Sam was at Boonville he became a Muslim. He read 'Muhammad Speaks' (the Muslim newspaper) and kept one with him all the time. When Sam came home he had changed. All the things he used to do, he stopped doing. Since he had killed Bow he stopped going to dances and clubs, he even stopped wearing fancy clothes. He became a political activist and a serious revolutionist. He started travelin' across the country, organizin' revolutionary-minded brothers. He met Rap Brown and they helped organize the Black Panther Party. They rode around the country speakin' at various colleges and universities. They were informing black students of how the U. S.

20

government was keeping black people enslaved, depressed, and without hope. The U. S. government, by denying blacks the opportunity for and equal education, better jobs and better housing, were continuing the racist practices that blacks were forced to endure. Sam and Rap Brown joined other black politicians who were concerned about black peoples' welfare.

They were helpin' to organize campaigns to get politicians elected to office who would help poor blacks live a better life. Sam first started helpin' Congressman Bill Clay. At this time, Sam was about nineteen years of age. About that time, Bill Clay and Adam Clayton Powell were some of the people who were speakin' up for black peoples' welfare and future. Matter of fact, Sam got in touch with Adam Clayton Powell and asked him to come to St. Louis to help protest against the way blacks were being discriminated against in education, jobs, and housing. Adam Clayton Powell came to St. Louis in 1968. The Black Liberators contacted the Ninth District Police Station and asked for protection for Mr. Powell. The request was denied. Therefore, the Black Liberators and Sam provided protection for him. The Black Liberators organized a protest march down Franklin, near their headquarters. Black Liberator members marched with real weapons and live ammo in their weapons. These were brothers who were dedicated to the Cause, ready to fight and give their lives, in order to improve and uplift humanity.

The original members of the Black Liberators were: Sam Petty, Charles Koen, Leon Dent, Cliff Valentine, Waldale Dobelly, Frank Washington, Leon Roberson, and Oscar King; Sam was the founder and later made a general. Sam was a natural-born leader. One of the members, Oscar King, turned out to be an informant.

Black Liberator members patrolled our neighborhoods to make sure that no one would bring any harm to families. If we caught anyone robbin' anyone, breakin' into houses, or raping a sister, we would beat their ass so bad, I guarantee you that they would not do it again. Sometimes the rapist would get raped in return. Sometimes we would torture them. Back in them days, we would leave our doors open and never worry about anyone comin' in our homes and stealin' anything. We knew everyone in our neighborhood, including their cars.

The Black Liberators began catchin' some heat from Ninth District police officers. They attempted to make it seem as if the Black Liberators were running a crime organization or were attempting to take over our neighborhoods. Since the police would not provide protection for our neighborhood, we provided it ourselves. Once we began this action, we began to see more things that needed to be done. Things like improving living conditions by fixing up our run-down houses, improving street lights, improving the education for our children, and providing jobs for our People. The System was not doing these things for our people because it was a part of their plan to keep us down and hopeless. The System wanted our neighborhoods to become crime infested and poverty stricken, ensuring that blacks were trapped with nowhere to find relief. Blacks would continue killin' each other. This was the System's long-range plan for poor blacks and our neighborhoods.

Back then, the black woman did not have to worry about food for their children because the System provided the basic needs for survival. But our living and other conditions suffered because of our poverty. The fathers had no jobs to help out with their families. Therefore he had to steal, or hustle, the best way he could.

This was the white man's way of destroying the black family and keeping them in poverty. We would end up in prison or the graveyard. The bottom line was that there would not be a father at home to help raise the sons and the black man's family would continue to be locked in HELL!

I did not realize it then, but black folks were on their way to becomin' a powerful force and the System did not intend to let that happen. The System started to brutalize us until it was almost impossible for the black man to make any progress through legitimate channels.

Back in 1968 Leon Dent and Charles Keon were protesting against the injustices that blacks were cursed with. They were arrested by Ninth District police officers and while in their custody they were brutalized; victims of police brutality. Leon Dent was convicted and sentenced to the state penitentiary (Behind the Wall). All the Black Liberators ended up Behind the Wall, with the exception of Charles Keon. He moved to Cairo, Illinois, and organized another branch of the Black Liberators. They were in the same condition, as most poor black folk in America. My brother Sam had already been doing his thing. He had been spreading the word on how blacks had been denied the opportunity for a better life and that it was time to stand up for our rights by protesting and voting for those who would fight for our rights. During this time Sam had already hooked up with Rap Brown. It was during this time that he met the fiery Angela Davis.

During this time Joe and I were hangin' out together, real tough. We used to be together every day, especially in the Projects. That's when Joe met this girl, we called her Hot. Her real name was Evelyn. Joe and her started goin' together. I used to drop him off at Hot's in the Projects. I would then come back and get him at a certain time; I would never not come back to pick him up. My mother taught me if I left home with him I better come back with him or suffer the consequences, with that iron cord. Man! That ironing cord was no joke. So I was Joe's big brother and protector. Joe hated that, but he loved hanging out with me because he was getting a lot of pussy in the Projects. And no one would mess with him because I had established a reputation. If you messed with one of my brothers, you would have to deal with me. Joe had another girlfriend by the name of Tookie, which is what we called her. Her real name was Linda Williams. Joe had a son by her; his name was Daryle Williams. He had two girls by Hot, their names were Lachelle and Yolanda. Joe had a total of five girls and four boys, that I know of. One of Joe's sons got killed in East St. Louis, Illinois. Joe was the first one to start makin' babies among us. I was next; my first son was born in 1973 and my oldest daughter was born in 1973. Both these children had different mothers. All total I have five sons and two daughters, that I know of. Sam has one son and one daughter.

Back in 1966 when I got out of Boonville, I had not changed. I went back to my old neighborhood, doing the same things I was doing before I was committed. Then one day I was arrested for carrying a concealed weapon. I was locked down in the City Jail on Fourteenth Street. I stayed there for about eight months. I eventually plea bargained to the concealed weapons charge and was sentenced to a year in the City Workhouse in 1967. The judge gave me about eight months jail time off my Workhouse sentence. So, I did four months. Man! City Jail was a bitch. We did not have any air conditioning. We also had to wash our own clothes by hand, or your family had to drop you clean clothes off, during a certain time of the week. The food was horrible; you ate it to stay alive. They had a commissary wagon that came around every day. It had lots of junk food on it, along with hygiene items. You could use jail money to purchase merchandise from the commissary wagon. You could withdraw jail money from your account at certain times. Jail money was made out of metal. It came in coins of one dollar, fifty cents, twenty-five cents, ten cents, and five cents. The tier man kept transactions under control on the tier.

The tier man made sure that all the inmates got along without fighting one another. Most of the tiers that I spent time on, I was the tier man. A tier man had to be a strong person, who really knew how to handle his self, or the other inmates would run over him. When a fight broke out, the tier man would be the one that broke it up and kept the peace. Inmates who were weak relied on the tier man to keep them from getting robbed of their money from their account or they received something on a visit. Sometimes, the tier man would keep them from getting raped, but everyone didn't get saved. Some inmates put their money in this bag we had. This money was used to help the five or six dudes, who helped the tier man keep things in order. Sometimes we ran into some pretty big dudes who refused to put their share in the bag. We would beat their ass and from then on, there were no more problems. However, we did make sure that they received soap, toothpaste, and deodorant.

Those inmates who were child molesters and snitches were treated harshly, especially those who snitched against their partners in crime. No one liked a person who broke weak and snitched his partner out. It was believed by those who were true to the game that if you were man enough to commit the crime, you should be man enough to handle the punishment. Many of the inmates who got the Treatment never came back to jail again.

My name was ringing throughout the City Jail. There were guards who did not like me and some that did. Many inmates who got the Treatment were callin' my name when they left the tier. Guards that did not like me moved me to another tier. They were hopin' that someone on that tier would beat my ass. These guards had already set me up to get assaulted by inmates on that tier.

At this time I was about eighteen; I was six-one, and weighing about two hundred and five pounds. This was considered a big dude. My jailing outfit consisted of bib overalls, a sweat shirt, and penny boots. When I was moved to another tier, I would put my mattress over my head so the inmates could not see who I was until I got all the way on the tier. That's when I threw the mattress off my head. The inmates would be hollering "Come on in here, nigger, we gonna' get into that ass.' When they saw who I was, they were saying "Lorenzo Baba, what's up?" Then the guards who thought they were setting me up for an ass beating would say "Damn!" Before you knew it, I was runnin' that tier.

Back in those days, we were on lock down twenty-four hours a day, sometimes kept on the fifth floor. The guards would let us out back, where we were housed. They would also let us use the bullpen area to hang out, sometimes to play cards.

Man! Nine months in that City Jail would drive you crazy if you didn't have a strong mind. I helped a lot of inmates make it by including them in my exercise program and discussing the law regarding crime and punishment. Most inmates that I did time with did not know anything about the state laws. The state was in the practice of leaving inmates in the City Jail for a long time, in order to get them to plea bargain their cases. This practice was contrary to the statue dealing with a speedy trial. All the state was interested in was a conviction.

I was sentenced to a year in the City Workhouse in 1967. I got out in November of 1967. In January of 1968 I got a job at Hubble Metals company with the help of the Jeff Vander Lou organization. I had been working there about three months when my brother Joe got shot. One day we were walking through the neighborhood. I stopped on Jefferson and Cass. Joe said "I'm going home." I said "Okay." I had stopped to talk to some brothers and sisters. Soon after that, I heard about nine shots ring out. I looked to see where the shots were fired from; I didn't see anything so I continued kicking it, until this girl came running up to me saying "Joe just got shot!" I ran to where I thought Joe was. When I got there, Joe was laid out on the ground. I asked him where he was hit. He told me, in the stomach, and in his right foot. The bullet that hit his right foot had broken the bones in that foot and he couldn't walk. Some dude had stopped and asked if he could help. He happened to have a car. He put Joe in his car and took him to Homer G. Phillips Hospital. They operated to remove the bullet from his stomach. Come to find out, Joe had shot himself by accident. This worried me, because it was his second time he had been shot in the stomach. But Joe was young and that was on his side. Joe stayed in Homer G. for about two weeks before he came home. While he was in the hospital we were worried about someone comin' up in the hospital to finish him off. So we gave him a pistol for protection and we went to the hospital every day, friends and family. Sam and myself were never without our pistols especially after Joe got shot. In the past we would not always carry pistols, only to the places where we thought we might need them. But after that shooting we kept them on us all the time. Man! We were mad as hell about Joe getting shot and it hurt because Joe was our little brother. Plus, Joe and I were real close, and I had a real bad temper. I was determined to find the people who were responsible for shooting Joe. Shit like that, you could not let go. If you did not get satisfaction, people would think you were soft and someone else would try it. We may have not needed them, but after that shooting we kept our pistols on us around the clock.

My family was a family you couldn't do something to and get away with it. We would get satisfaction, sooner or later, making things right; that was guaranteed.

What really started this shootin' with Joe was and incident where some people got robbed in the West End area. The people who got robbed told this dude name Jim that some dude from downtown, from the North Side, had robbed them. Jim's family lived in Pruitt-Igoe, where Jim was living at the time. No one really knew where he was raised. He just popped up one day in the Projects. When someone told Jim that someone had robbed them, Jim told them, "If the Petty boys didn't do it, they probably knew who did."

One day while my brother Joe and another person was standing on the corner of Leffingwell and Cass, a car pulled up and parked. This dude Jim got out and started walking towards Joe. He had a gun in his hand. Then suddenly Joe said a shot was fired, then Jim jumped back in the car, and the car sped off, with Jim and some other dudes inside. Joe had said that he didn't know who the other dudes were until he got shot on Cass. We didn't know anything about them. One day, this dude came up to us and said this dude name Jim was going around telling people he was going to kill us. This dude asked Jim "What did they do to you?" Jim would not say. This dude said he told Jim "Man, them dudes ain't no pussies." We also had several other people tell us that Jim had said the same thing to them.

One day while Joe was in the hospital, I was walking around on Franklin looking for some of my friends. I didn't have a car at the time. When I left off Franklin, I was being followed but didn't realize it until I got to Leffingwell and Gamble. I had looked over my shoulder and saw a car with this dude hanging out the front passenger window. He had a gun in his hand. He shot at me about six times. I took cover and pulled my piece. I got off about six shots at the car as it turned on Dayton.

I then went home, which was about five blocks away. I told this old dude from the neighborhood about what had happened. He told me if I didn't get a car and stop walking the streets, they were going to kill me. So, the first check I got from my job, I bought me a car. I bought me another good gun with the next check. My brother Joe and I eventually had a shoot-out with Jim—he lost. We ended up Pleadin' out. I was arrested on my job at Hubbell Metals company and locked down in City Jail for about nine months. James Bell was my attorney at the time. Joe and I were sentenced to the State Penitentiary, Behind the Wall, in Jefferson City. H-Hall was our first stop. That's where they put all new inmates, for classification. You were there for about thirty days until it was decided at which prison you would do your time. Until then, you were locked down, and isolated from the general population. We were allowed out of our cells only when we went to the commissary, which was at least once a month.

My brother and I were in the same cell until we were transferred. They sent Joe to Algoa and I was sent to Moberly. We were both transferred in January of 1969. I was placed in One House, at Moberly. At that time Moberly had only two houses; they had started to build Three House, but I wasn't there when they finished.

When I went to prison, my reading and writing were on a fourth-grade level. I got schooling at Moberly; the teachers were not that good, but I hung in there. Later on I got into welding and took a small engine repair class. When I completed that, I enrolled in and electronics class, but I never completed it, as I started gettin' into black history with some more brothers. We changed our names; I changed mine to Zola, which meant to love. That black History class was the turning point in my learning to read better.

We got together anywhere we could, taking turns reading from a black history book. Many black inmates could not read as well as others. Those who were better readers helped those who needed help. The black history classes helped black inmates make progress. But then the administration felt that we were making too much progress and they transferred me and other inmates to other prisons, for fear of other inmates joinin' us. We were learning more outside the classroom, than inside the classroom. Inmates were teaching other inmates better than the teachers who had been hired.

They sent me Behind the Wall, where they sent all hard and dangerous inmates in January of 1970. I was twenty-nine at the time.

Many of the inmates Behind the Wall were from St. Louis and Kansas City, Missouri. I knew a lot of inmates from St. Louis, from my hood and City Jail. Inmates Behind the Wall were doing big time. Many were doing life and didn't give a damn about anybody especially if you disrespected them or got in their business; they would do very serious harm to you. I witnessed many stabbings over Gay Boy, and debts. Back then money Behind the Wall was cigarettes. If you gave and inmate ten packs of cigarettes, they owed you fifteen packs back. I never smoked cigarettes but I had a cigarette store. That's how I made my living Behind the Wall. I was poor and my mother was on welfare. Most of the time she could not afford to send me any money. Every now and then she managed to send me twenty-five dollars. I also worked in the kitchen as a cook. I was selling sandwiches for a pack or sometimes two of ciga-rettes, dependin' on the type of sandwich it was.

I stopped working in the kitchen and started working in the laundry. We washed sheets, bedspreads, and inmate's laundry bags. If you didn't have a personal laundry man your clothes would come up missing. Everyone who worked in the laundry had their own personal customers. Everyone got paid a certain price per bag; it depended on the size of the load. I charged about five packs of squares a bag. I had about ten customers, which came to about five cartons. Back then, five cartons was a lot of money. Plus, I would let certain inmates borrow smokes from me. In some cases, if you borrowed a carton, you would owe me fifteen packages. I was always turning my money over—that's the way I survived. I had no one else to depend on. You couldn't ask anyone for anything, because they would want to play some kind of game on you. The main game they tried to play was getting you to be their Gay Boy when you couldn't pay them back. Man! Prison was cold-blooded. The inmates you thought were your friends were the ones you had to watch out for.

While I was Behind the Wall, my brother Joe got rolled from Moberly to Behind the Wall. We were together for about six months. I was then sent to L-Hall, which was right outside the Wall. I hated to leave Joe by himself. But there were many inmates Behind the Wall from St. Louis who respected me and Joe. But no one wanted a problem with and inmate who would come at your ass if you tried to harm him or his family. I also had a family of friends who were cold-blooded killers. My family was well known and we had looked out for fellow inmates when they needed it the most.

Joe made it home safe; however he was picked up and taken to a juvenile facility where he had to do time on a sawn-off gun case. He had caught this case before he got charged in the murder of Jim. Joe got out around 1971. He went to work as a substitute teacher at this school that was located on Evans.

While Joe was home free I was still locked down in Jeff City. I was still in L-Hall, and was playin' on the basketball team. We traveled to different places and played other teams. One day we went Behind the Wall to play a game. After we finished playing, we left through the control tower. After we exited through the front door, we were walking towards L-Hall, which was right down the street. When we got to L-Hall, we were called back Behind the Wall, by Warden Warwick. He lined all of us up and asked who was the one who said "hey baba" to the white woman who was outside the building when we left. No one said anything because we didn't know what he was talking about. We never saw any white woman when we left from Behind the Wall. Then the warden went down the line and started to point out people. He picked about six inmates and told the rest to go back to L-Hall. I was one of the six that Warden Warwick picked to remain. He and Captain Deerhoff took us to his office. Warden Warwick asked us again, "who said it?" No one said anything. Everyone was scared to death but me. I told the warden, "We didn't see anyone outside, when we left." He said, "I thought I recognized your voice." He told all the inmates to go back to the Hall, but he made me stay. Once everyone had left, the warden tried to spray Mace in my face. I ducked, and covered my face with my hands. Then the warden and Captain Deerhoff started beating me in the back of my head, on my arms and on my back with their fists. They took me Behind the Wall. While going there, they continued beating me. Captain Deerdoff was also kicking me in the ass with his pointed-toe cowboy boots. They then took me to the Hole. Back then, the Hole was under B-Hall. They put me in a thin jump suit and gave me a real thin mattress to sleep on. Back then you had to sleep on the floor as there were no beds in the Hole. I stayed in the Hole for about two weeks. Everyday Boguard and Mace Man (who were guards) would come to the Hole to jump on me. They were trying to make me confess that I said had said "Hey baba" to that white woman. Man! The back of my head, back, and arms were sore from them guys beating on me for two weeks.

This type of brutality continued until my mother came to visit me. When I came out in this jump suit, my mother asked me, what I was doing in it. I told her what they were doing to me. She then said, "What?" She then said, "I'll get this shit straighten out." She got up, left the visiting room and went to the Governor's Mansion, which was located near the Penitentiary. She wanted to speak with the governor about my situation.

She waited there for about six hours before she could see him. When the governor decided to see her, she introduced herself and showed him her certificate that she had received from him for nineteen years of service working on the voting polls. After seeing her certificate, he asked what the problem was. She told him about her son Behind the Wall, who was being beaten. He told her not to worry about it, because he would handle it, and he did. They came the next day and let me out the Hole.

I was then transferred to Church Farm and put to work in the dairy where I milked cows. I had to get up around 4:00 A.M. and was finished around 6:00 A.M. We then were taken to breakfast. Every morning we had bacon and eggs for breakfast. After breakfast we got off until evening. We then had to go back to the dairy and milk more cows getting off around 5:30 P.M. We then ate dinner where we were allowed to eat as much as we could.

I stayed at Church Farm for about eight or nine months. They sent me to the Farm about February of 1971. When I got there they were cuttin' down trees. All year long we were on some kind of work detail. In March of '71 we started planting seeds and small flowers, along with vegetables in a big field. Man, it was hot as hell in those fields. The fields were so long you couldn't see the end of the rows. The key to getting some rest was whoever got to the end first could rest until everyone else finished their row. It took all day for some to finish their row. Me and my friends had gotten into pretty good shape, but we had to drink lots of water.

Around July we started pulling vegetables out of the ground and loading them on the truck. We did that work up until August and then we went to the Factory, where we cleaned the vegetables and put them in cans. Every day before we came out of the fields, the boss would let me run behind the truck back to the farm, which about one mile. I told him I was boxing, that's why I wanted to run, he said yes. My friend from St. Louis, named Hat, was the driver of the truck. His real name was Johnnell Whitterton. Sometimes Hat's foot would get kind of heavy on the gas, which made me run about fifteen to twenty miles per minute. When Hat stopped, I would say, "Man! What you trying to do, kill me?" I had to keep up with the truck because if I didn't make it back with the crew, I could be charged with escape—that made me run hard. When we made it back to the Farm he had count. After that we had dinner and then we went behind the house unit, to play handball. Man! We had some energy. It seem like we would be tired after coming out of the field. My man Hat was my best friend at Ranch Farm. We started lending money to inmates and they were paying back us back with Commissary Money Books. They came in 3, 4, 5, 10 and 15 dollar stamps. We had so many books until someone told the People we were taking inmates' Money Books, which we were not. We were making interest off our money and some inmates didn't like it. We had everything we wanted.

One night around 11:00 P.M., the guard came around and got Hat and me. We were scared to death. Usually, when they transfer you for something like that, they usually jump on you. But, this time they didn't do it. They put us in the Hole for about two weeks. That was in November of '71. When I came out they put me in C-Hall, which had one-man cells. In May of '72, I went home from Jeff City. I couldn't wait to get out because I wanted to sell some dope, so I could make me some big money.

Before I got out, we talked about how to become better criminals. No one ever talked about how to start some kind of business, or where a life of crime would lead and the consequences. If someone had told me that I could accomplish the same material things doing it that way: working for it, I wouldn't have had to worry about losing my freedom and spending all my life locked down in prison. I had to learn the hard way. Because I learned the hard way, I've learned to appreciate the LITTLE things in life. These things I have found to be more important and more MEANINGFUL! Freedom and PEACE of MIND are more valuable than a whole lot of money. My family is more important than any material thing.

In May of '72 I was released from Behind the Wall. Joe came to pick me up. His friend Butchie was with him. Butchie was wheeling a brand-new 98 Olds. They were rolling with lots of good sounds. When we started rolling towards St. Louis, Joe fired up a joint. I laid back and enjoyed the first day of my freedom. Joe also put $600 in my pocket. As we rode through the streets of Jeff City, I was checkin' out everything. Everything was looking good. I was truly happy to be out of prison.

I had no intentions of gettin' a job. While locked down, all we talked about was committing crimes, especially selling dope. All my friends and associates were into the fast, big-money game out there. But nobody was telling us about the consequences connected with drug trafficking, how much time you were facing in prison. Most of the inmates Behind the Wall were doing time for murder, robbery, or rape. They were not qualified to tell us about the one-way dead-end road connected with dealing drugs.

Hustlin' was a way of life for me. I came up hustlin—it was the way I survived. I started stealing early in life. The Coca-Cola Company was one of my favorite hustles. The company was located in the neighborhood on Magazine close to where we lived. Man, we use to steal cases of coke, and sell them for a dollar a case. If we had a couple of dollars in our pockets, we had enough money to buy something to eat and drink. Hustlin' was in my blood.

When I got out of prison in 1972, Joe took me to this clothing store on West Florissant. This is where I met Mose Lee Wallace and Jimmy Coopwood. They were in the clothing business and friends of Sam and H. Rap Brown. These brothers let me get some clothing on credit. I ordered about $1,800 worth of clothing before we left the store. We then went visiting brothers we knew around the city that we knew were doing good. Everyone I saw put money in my pocket; two, three hundred dollars. This was good money, but not enough to do what I wanted to do. I then started looking around town to see who I could buy some dope from. Back in them days, everybody wasn't handling any large amounts of drugs, and not just anybody could buy large amounts of drugs. You had to be well known to buy quantities of dope. You also had to be a brother with a reputation for shooting that pistol.

Back then if you used dope, you couldn't buy it unless you grew up in the hood. Dealers thought you were a snitch or the police. If you were under twenty-one, you couldn't buy dope from anyone. Also, no one would let you sell dope. My dope business was mainly downtown on the North Side in the Zone 6 area. That's where I grew up. My brother Joe had his people who were dealing.

Once things got started my people were rolling, the money was coming in big time. Joe was beginning to have problems collecting his money from his people. I had heard about it. He had started pistol whipping and threatening to do more if his money didn't get right. I decided to bring Joe into my operation before he got hurt. That would really hurt me. We went 50-50, cutting the profits down the middle. He was now getting money like I was. That's when we started buying big luxury rides, dressing in the finest, and wearing expensive jewelry.

We then began steppin' out on the town. One of our favorite spots was the High Note Lounge on Delmar. The owner Squeaky was cool people. Her son Michael was also cool. She had a brother, Leroy Hawkshaw. This brother was down and I learned a lot from him about the game of life. I began going there on a regular basis, because A. Q., aka Arthur Qualls, was a friend of mine, and that was one of his favorite spots. Arthur was also one of the major drug dealers in St. Louis. There were many other well-known blacks with status who hung out at the High Note. Arthur and Leroy were pimpin' when the game was fading for black pimps. Black Zep, too, was pimpin' major league. His whores were mostly white girls, his favorite. The McIntosh brothers also were hangin' out at the High Note. This family was one of the most respected and feared families in downtown black St. Louis. The Davis brothers, Earl and Sammy, made the High Note their favorite hangout. T. J. Ruffin was a well-known brother who enjoyed the High Note on a regular basis.

I first met A. Q. when I was doin' time in Jeff City. He and I trained promising boxers. We met at Church Farm in '71 when I was at Moberly. One day we all met Behind the Wall for a boxing tournament. This was the first time I met A. Q. I had heard of him, but we had never met. When we met, we began talking, and Arthur asked me if I got high. I said yes.

Back then, we were getting high off mace. Mace was a high like weed, but it came in powder form, which was used in pies and cakes. It would get you high, as long as you were drinking something hot, like coffee or hot Tang. We drank both of them and stayed high for about twenty-four hours.

Arthur had mace for me when we got together at boxing events. I then started bringing him a high whenever we got together at a boxing event. Sometimes we would have something different for each other. A. Q. and I became real cool. When I got home, A. Q. and me started hangin' out at some of the nicer places. Everywhere we went, many of the people there were hangin' out with us because we were gettin' high and gettin' everybody around us high. We were always buying each other drinks.

Back then, we were running the West End. We knew everybody who was getting money and they had people behind them that were known and would shoot that pistol. We were one big family. We had good times and lived very well.

After the High Note closed, Joe Coates opened J. C.'s Get Up Lounge on Whittier and Lindell. Man! That was the spot. Some of the most beautiful black women in St. Louis loved J. C.'s. However, they were just followin' that dollar. The dudes who hung out in J. C.'s had that dollar.

The first time I met Joe Coates was in J. C.'s. That too was the first time I met Jerry Brown, Sr. These two brothers were major players in assorted enterprises, big-money businesses. Man! Them brothers had class. They really knew how to dress and treat women. Everyone who hung out at J. C.'s, had money and treated the women to drinks all the time. All the brothers that frequented J. C.'s respected each other. Everyone who was known in the Game throughout the city was hanging in J. C.'s. We too, were hangin' out at Maurice's Gold Coast, off of Lindell and Compton. It was across the street from the LaClede Town housing project. Man! Maurice's was a cool spot. Lots of well-known people hung out there. Plus, Maurice was a personal friend of mine. The Voyager was another club that we visited down the street from Maurice's. It too, was a real cool spot. We also use to go to the Regal Sports Lounge also down the street from Maurice's. It was a cool spot as well. Later on, the Regal Sports was renamed Andrea's. There was a club on Olive Street named the Palace. This spot was really jumpin'. All up and down Olive between Whittier and Sarah, there were numerous clubs and places to eat. This area was known as Gaslight Square.

In addition to the clubs and eating establishments, there was another BOOMING business. Prostitution was wide open on streets like Olive, Delmar, Sarah, Washington, and Lindell. This area was known as the Hoe Stroll, it was hoppin'! The Levine Rose on Jefferson and Cass was another spot that was popular. On Sunday they sold alcohol and food. This was especially the spot for the neighborhood hang-out. Also, lots of dope was being sold in this neighborhood around Elliot, Sheridan, Glasgow, Garrison, and Benton.

The Pruitt-Igoe projects was bordered by Jefferson, 19th Street, and Carr Drive. There was lots of dope being sold out of the Projects. But not just anybody could sell dope in the Projects. Certain people ran it. Everywhere else, anyone who was respected in their hood and had a reputation for shootin' that pistol could deal. Plus, not just anyone could buy dope. You had to be from that hood. Outsiders could not buy dope unless he was known, or someone from that hood had to buy it for them. Then, they had to take care of the person that had copped for them. Back in the day, a person under 21 couldn't buy dope from anyone. They couldn't even sell dope in certain areas. We wouldn't sell dope in front of people's homes. We would deal from a house we had rented from a lot, or from the alley.

Everything started to look up in 1973. My mother bought a two-story building at 4256 College Avenue. Downstairs was a store-front. Upstairs was and apartment where my mother ended up living. Downstairs, I opened a grocery store. I had to clean everything out of the downstairs section. I also had one of the walls torn down to make more room. I then had another section built onto the back of the store; it was the meat department.

The store started doing very good. Later on we added a liquor department. My mother ran it. She really loved running the liquor department because she loved dealing with people. My brother Joe and I ran the store. However, when I first opened the store, Joe didn't want any part of it. But when he saw how good the store was doing, he wanted to be part owner. I took Joe in because I didn't want anything to happen to him in the streets.

In 1975 I bought a house in North Florissant in the County located at 1321 Aspen Dr. At the time there were only two or three black families in that area and I was one of them. Joe bought a home in Norwood in 1975 after I bought mine. He never wanted me to out-do him. Joe always had good taste.

Things were looking up for both of us. Sam was still locked down in a New York prison in '75. He had caught a case in '71 and wasn't cut loose until '76.

We visited Sam while he was doin' time. Joe and I would go visit him every ninety days. We would leave him $400 apiece. Plus we were putting $30 a day away at the store for Sam when he came home.

When Sam came home Joe and I drove to the airport and picked him up in a new 1976 Cadillac Seville. Sam had caught a case with H. Rap Brown in 1971. They had been convicted of robbery, assault, and attempted murder. There were other co-defendants charged with them. These other brothers were Levi Valentine and Arthur Jones. These brothers had been in New York City to stop the dope sales to and by young people. Young dope dealers, who were convicted of selling drugs were not receiving the time that adult dealers were. There was also a problem with the number of young people who were over-dosing from heroin in the city. Sam and Rap Brown didn't like it at all. They decided to do something about it. But in the process, they were charged with about seven robberies, assaults, and attempted murder.

Sam went to trial; Joe and I got him a lawyer. His name was William McKinley. Rap Brown's attorney was William Counselor. Both lawyers fought very hard for Sam and Rap Brown.

38

Sam had a watch on his arm when they arrested him. One of the witnesses against them said the watch was his. Sam declared that the watch belonged to him. Back at home, my mother had the receipt from where Sam had bought the watch. We gave his attorney a copy of the receipt.

Sam's attorney started bullshitting with his case. Sam was having a hard time getting him to come and visit him. Sam called the store and told us about it. Joe and I went to New York to find his lawyer. First we went to visit Sam. He told us where we could find him. It was right down the street from the New York City Jail. Sam told us that every day, attorney McKinley was at this lounge, having a drink. The next day around noon, Joe and I went to pay him a visit. I really didn't know what he looked like. But I knew how lawyers usually dressed. When we walked in the lounge I looked around and I saw this dude, who looked like he could be him. We walked up to him and asked him, was he attorney McKinley. He said yes. I introduced myself. I told him I was Sam Petty's brother and that Sam told me that he had not seen him in about three months. I also told him that Sam needed to talk with him about his case and that it was very important. He told me he would go to see Sam, but not right then. When he said that, I showed him my pistol and told him that he was goin' right then, or I was going to leave his body right there. He got the message. We all walked down the street to the jail. We walked into the jail and went to the front desk. There was a black female officer there. I told her who I wanted to see. She then told me to take off my sunglasses so she could hear what I was saying. Once I pulled them off, she said, "Now I can hear you." For a minute I was scared, because I had the pistol on me and I wasn't about to let anyone arrest me. Things worked out; Sam and his lawyer talked. We left New York and returned to St. Louis. After we returned to St. Louis, we had to get back on our job, which was operating our store. Our store was opened every day at 8:00 A.M. This operation included bringing merchandise up from the basement. We then cleaned the store, especially the meat department. We did this every night. People knew that we had a very clean store.

Durin' this time my mother's health started goin' down to the point that she was unable to run the liquor business. She had cancer, and it was really eatin' her up. She started losing a lot of weight and she didn't want to eat. She passed away in 1975. Joe and I were in the streets when she passed away; Sam was still locked down in New York. He was not allowed to attend her funeral.

Sam came home from Danamor in 1976. Joe and I picked him up from Lambert Airport. We were riding in my new 1976 Seville Cadillac. Joe was driving. I was riding shotgun. And O'Jays tape was jammin'. We fast-forwarded to our "Family Reunion," when we put Sam in the backseat. Man! That was the first time we were together on the streets since 1968. It was a good feeling for us to see each other and be together.

Joe and I had the store rolling. We both were doing very good. We both gave Sam three grand apiece. Sam had been paroled home to our store. Now we were all working together.

Sam bought the first Dollar House in the City of St. Louis. Things were looking up for Sam. He had run up on some furniture for his new house and moved right on in. Barbara had a daughter from her first marriage. In the back of his house he built a brick garage. It was two stories.

After Sam finished his house, we began fixing up old, run-down houses on the North Side. The first piece of property that we started renovating was on Pope at the corner of West Florissant. It was a two-family structure. I purchased that property from an old man. He had seen me standing outside, looking at it. He had asked me if I was interested in buying it. He told me if I was interested, he could give me a good price. I asked what was the price. He said, "What about $3,500?" He then took me inside to look at it. It wasn't in that bad of shape. I ended up putting about seven grand more into the property.

But by the time we were finished with the house, I was in jail. We had started working on the property in 1977. I was arrested in 1978. Before I was arrested, some individuals came to my store and attempted to kill me. They attempted to make it look like a robbery but it was really a planned hit.

That night I and my brother were working alone. I had let everyone else go early as a treat, for having done such a good job. I was working behind the counter, waiting on lots of customers. Joe was in the back, cutting meat for some customers.

Sometime later, I was by myself. While taking care of my customers, I noticed three dudes on the outside of the store. They had weapons and ski masks on. They rushed in the store. I shouted out to my customers "Down!" I then dove behind the counter, at the same time pulling out my pistol. I stuck my hand over the counter and let all eight rounds go. The three had made it to the counter. I then snatched my shotgun, jumped over the counter, and laid on the floor. The three had run from the store. I crawled from the store. When I got outside, I got on one knee. The first thing I saw was a red car doubled parked, with the front door opened; it had white interior. When I saw the lights come on, I opened fire. I heard the radiator bust. I then saw another car backing down the street with the lights off. I started firin' at it. I was firin' at anything that moved. I fired a shotgun blast at the lounge across the street from my store.

The fact that I had pushed the robbery button was on my side. The police came right away from every direction. They asked me what happened. I told them. By the time I finished telling them what had happened, other police had arrived on the scene. One of police cars had two dudes in the car. The police asked me if I could identify them as those who tried to rob me. I told them no, because they had on ski masks. One officer insisted that I take a good look. When I did, I realized I knew them both. They were Brother D's people. Right away, I knew who was involved. Then one of the policemen said that one of the cars that was outside my store belonged to Brother D's girlfriend. Then the police told me that when he got the robbery alert on his radio, he spotted these two guys running down the street. When he searched for them, he found them hiding under a porch. He said he knew they were involved.

The police started bringing guns into my store, putting them on the floor. They also were finding more weapons outside the store and in the street. Man! They brought in about fifteen guns. I said "Damn! I didn't know that there were that many people out there." I sent a friend to the liquor store to buy me a big bottle of MD 20-20 wine. My nerves got real bad and I needed a drink. Then one officer told me if he wasn't on duty, he would have a drink with me, because this wasn't a robbery. Someone had come to kill me. I started preparing to protect myself. I was ready to defend myself, my family, and my business. They had declared war on us.

In 1978 the FBI arrested me for conspiracy to distribute narcotics. I was framed. They wanted to take me off the streets because they had no other way to stop the war. They used and informant by the name of Robert Russell to lie on me. The first sale the FBI charged me with took place on Harper Street. They used Robert Russell and another dude who was acting like he was me. Then they used Robert to buy drugs from Levi Valentine on several occasions. After they had gotten Levi, they had Robert call my store, to talk to me. At the time Robert was hustling and selling all kinds of shit. He was trying to buy some candy apples from my store, which he never did before. They used that phone conversation as a narcotics distribution conversation and arrested me.

While Levi and I were in the St. Clair County Jail the FBI got Levi to cooperate with them by saying he got his drugs from me. Once they got Levi to say that I accepted a plea bargain. I was thinking that I was going to get seven or eight years. However, I was sentenced to fifteen years. This was the maximum sentence that I could have received if I had gone to trial. I could not have received anything more than fifteen years when they arrested me on the drug charge. I was also charged with possession of a firearm that I had on me when they arrested me. I was thinking that the sentences were supposed to run concurrent. They forced me to have a judge rule on the weapons charge. I was given a two-year sentence on the weapons charge. The charges were to be served consecutively in a federal prison. They gave me a ten year special parole in connection with the sentence. Also at this time, I had another gun case pending in state court.

When I was in St. Clair County Jail, we were allowed one visit a week for fifteen minutes and one fifteen-minute telephone call a week. There were no T. V.s on the tiers. I stayed in St. Clair County Jail for about three months. They then sent me to Leavenworth Federal Penitentiary in Leavenworth, Kansas. Leavenworth was called The Big House. It is a maximum security prison where all the dangerous and notorious inmates are confined. While I was there, I saw several killings. This was very scary and made you have respect for other people, because you knew what could happen and how fast it could happen.

While I was doing time at Leavenworth, I went through lots of changes because I was broke. I was looking forward to my brothers sending me a few dollars every now and then. But it never happened from Sam. Joe would send me a $100.00 every ninety days. Joe and Sam were not getting along. Sam let Joe have the store; Joe started doing his own thing. Joe had sold his house and was now living in my house. I heard that Joe was using the money from the sale of the house to get high. He was broke in no time.

In December of 1982 I was transferred to the federal prison FCI, in Memphis, Tennessee. I was locked down there until December of 1988. After ten years in federal prison I was transferred to state prison to serve a three-year sentence. I spent my first thirty days in Fulton, Missouri. I then went to Algoa in 89. I was paroled from Algoa and transferred to Tipton, where I spent thirty days. From Tipton, I went to a halfway house in St. Louis, on Washington Avenue.

Jerry Brown, Sr. gave me a job, while I was in the halfway house. This helped me a great deal. I don't know what I would have done without J. B.'s help. He helped me get on my feet. Mr. Brown helped lots of brothers who needed help in their lives. Slowly but surely, I got myself together.

After checking out what was happening in the city, I checked out Sam's apartment buildings and how they had gone down. I decided to fix them up. Every dollar I got my hands on, I put back into those buildings.

One day I met this sister, Diane Moore. I remembered her from when she was coming down to City Jail to see this dude. I knew she was a good woman, because she was good to him. I decided to check her out, get to know her. We started datin' and got to know each other better. We then started going together. She began helping me with my apartment building. Before I got with Diane, I had been with my first wife, Pamela Miller. We had been married while I was locked down in Leavenworth. But after about four years together and coming to see me every month, she got tired and we divorced. When I came home we got back together, for a minute. We separated again, and that's when Diane and me got together. Diane helped me out a great deal. I was really able to get on my feet. Later Diane and I broke up. That's when I met Terry James. We started going together and everything was going smoothly between us.

One day I decided to go out to this firing range with this dude, Jesse. Terry had told me not to go, but I went anyway. This was in December of '91. This would be the last time I would see the streets for an eternity. I was arrested for bein' on the firing range with a gun. I went to trial on the gun charge. I was convicted and sentenced to seventeen years and eight months. I was then sent back to federal prison. This time I had to do eighty-five percent of the sentence, which totaled fifteen years and six months.

After being locked down in the Jennings County Jail for ninety days, I was transferred to the St. Clair County Jail where I stayed for about three months. It was winter time when I was locked down in Jennings. They kept the heat off in the cell area. This was they're way of breakin' you down and tellin' them what you knew and or arranging a plea. Man! I had to wear two pair of pants, long johns, and two pair of socks. I had four blankets on my bed and I used them all, day and night. Plus! We showered in cold water. It was so cold you could see your breath. When they transferred me to St. Clair, I was glad as hell. They had heat in St. Clair County Jail, thank God! However, the food there was rotten.

We had visits on Wednesday and Sunday for fifteen min-

44

utes. We went to the gym once a week. Sam and I were on the same tier together. This was a dormitory setting which housed about thirty prisoners. The living area was in back of the dorm area. The social recreation area was in the front of the dorm. This was where the telephone was located. Gaining access to the phone presented numerous concerns. Some prisoners took advantage by staying on the phone for long periods of time. Someone had to step up and urge the time abuser to get off the phone. Often telling the time abuser the phone was needed to make and important call to their lawyer or sick family member would do the trick. Most times, the abusers were crying to their girlfriends, begging them to hang in there and not to give up. Some of the prisoners couldn't even catch up with their women and that drove them crazy. Because they knew they were out somewhere, with another dude. Just the thought of an inmate's women out with another dude, would make many of the so-called strong dudes turn informants. Informants for the most part had it 'easy' as serving time went. They were given privileges that other prisoners weren't. Extra phone privileges were top-shelf privileges. Everybody couldn't handle confinement. Confinement could break down some of the most toughest inmates. The real bad times could drive an inmate to desperate measures.

Sam was doing a lot of reading during this period. He was fighting a big case. He and Jerry Lewis Bey were co-defendants in a federal drug case. Sam caught the case while he was in prison. He beat that case on two occasions. They made Sam and Jerry Lewis Bey co-defendants based on a telephone conversation they had on a prison phone Sam had been using. Sam fought this case for seven years before it was over. During this time Sam was locked down in just about every county jail in Missouri. He even spent a year in the Terre Haute Prison hold over.

I left the St. Clair County Jail after they sentenced me to the seventeen years and eight months. Sam was still fighting his case. In October of 1992 I was transferred to Memphis. In 1994 I was transferred to the Greenville Prison which had just been opened. I was the twentieth prisoner to step on the ground there. I worked as and orderly the whole time I was there. I spent six years at Greenville. While I was there I married Terry James. I was then transferred to the prison in Forest City, Arkansas, in 1998.

Now here it is July 2006 and I am scheduled to be released on December 12, 2007. I would have served fifteen years and six months, after being released from the halfway house.All total, I would have served 26 years 6 months in federal prison. I was now sixty years old.

While I was serving this seventeen-year sentence, I had time to think about many things that were said to me in the past, from my parents and older people, when I was growing up. My mother use to tell me how important an education is in this world, when it comes to getting a good job and not letting people beat you out of your money. They will, if you can't read or count. But at that time I thought I was such a great hustler that I didn't need an education. What I didn't think about or know was that hustlin' could get me killed or put in prison. I always thought that if I went to prison, my girlfriend and my so-called friends would be there for me. But it didn't turn out that way.

The first girlfriend I had in 1964 when I went to Boonville started going with one of my friends who they said looked a lot like me. My mother was there for me while I was doing that time. What I learned from that experience was that you could not put your trust in any women when it came to them being there for you while you were doing time.

When my mother was trying to get me to come in the house before it got dark I thought she was being a little too strict. I decided to act like I was grown and started staying out very late with my friends. While we were hanging out in the streets we were getting drunk, robbing and jumping on people. My mother knew this; that's why she was telling me to bring my ass in the house before it got dark. She knew about life in the ghetto and she knew young people got in trouble when they stayed out late at night, but I never listened. I was always trying to keep up with the crowd, and do what the crowd was doing. I didn't want anyone calling me scared. I was trying to impress on them that I wasn't scared when it came to getting high, fighting, robbing someone with a gun, or knocking them out with my hands. Every brother wanted to be the one with the most heart, because that's who got all the respect and attention; that's what it was all about; but I wasn't listening and didn't understand.

I'm sitting here trying to sum up my life, starting in 1978 when they took me off the street. I was twenty-nine years old. Man! My mind was tumblin'. I didn't have nobody to call on to ask no questions. They took my phone and took me off to a place, somewhere, shit! I couldn't get to no phone to tell nobody where I was. I had to wait until they let me use the phone. They done kidnapped me. They done everything to me, but blindfold me. Where was they takin' me? They didn't have to blindfold me because they was driving so goddamn fast, I couldn't recognize nothin', nowhere. You hear about all the stories in history how they rode off with people and they end up shot in the head on the side of the road somewhere. Everything was going through my mind, ain't no use me lying. Damn! I done got convicted. I done lost my store, which I had for about seven years. I had been rollin' on the top, man. Then they give me this time.

When I arrived at Leavenworth, I was nutty as a fruitcake. It started when I was in St. Clair County Jail. Man, when I went in front of this judge and he said 218 months. Man! I couldn't figure that out. I couldn't count that fast at all. My mind, my mathematics, boy, my mind just went blank. I stopped countin', couldn't count no more, you know. Lord, have mercy! What's goin' on here, what's he saying. He went on talking about when I got out the pen I was going to be so old, I was going to need a cane, crutches, or wheelchair. I said, oh yeh.

So I went on to Leavenworth. They were giving out paroles. I went to see the Parole Board in 1980. I was supposed to be doing about six years and some change if I didn't get in no trouble. I pulled about six years, ain't got in no trouble. They denied me and gave me two more years for being me. I went back up in eight years, was denied again. They said see you in two years. Shit! In 17 years, all I had to do was 10. So, I did the whole flat 10. Came up for Special Parole, but they dropped that because they said Special Paroles only applied to violent crimes. Distribution of drugs and conspiracy to distribute drugs were not violent crimes.

Now I'm in Leavenworth Penitentiary, serving 17 years. Leavenworth is located in Leavenworth, Kansas. It houses every bit of nine, ten, or eleven thousand inmates. They call Leavenworth the Big House. Anything can go down there. It is recognized as one of, if not the toughest prisons throughout the prison systems in America; and definitely the most dangerous in the federal system. The one before Leavenworth was Marion Penitentiary, located in Illinois. Now it's the penitentiary in Florence, Colorado. It's up there, where it's cold! You don't come out of your cell but for one hour a day; you're locked down for twenty-three.

In Leavenworth when you come out your cell, all movement is on the hour, every hour. You got five minutes to get to where you gotta go. Now can you imagine when you walk out in that hallway, you seeing about six, seven thousand-something people, constantly moving like little ants.

You got so many nigguhs up there, that be stabbin' you and hittin' you in the back of the head. You don't know who is who, so you gotta keep three or four dudes with you. When you sat break, everybody moves, ain't no foot draggin', ya dig. You be movin' so fast through that crowd, if somebody was tryin' to stick or hit you from the back, you a hard target. So that's how you lived and survived at Leavenworth, in a crowd. It was a mind-changer, man.

I was at Leavenworth with some of my best friends. Sylvester Akins, Arthur Quales, Leroy Hawkshaw, Robert and Fingers McIntyre and Big Quick. They were all there when I got there, all from St. Louis. Man! There were so many dudes from St. Louis up there; I guess they said welcome to the club.

While I was making out my visiting list I must have put

down about fifteen people. They were all the people that I knew I had looked out for before I came to Leavenworth; put them on their feet. If it wasn't for me, they wouldn't be where they was at, you know. Sylvester Akins said, "Man! One year from now, Jack, you won't be hearin' from none of them. Man, me and that dude fell out. I said "What you say!" He said "I ain't trying to make you mad at me, but a year from now, you ain't going to hear from damn near half on that list." I stopped talking to that dude for damn near a whole year.

That year went by an, it came to be. He was right. I didn't hear from nobody. There was three of us. Me, Sam, and Joe. Joe came to see me 'bout every six months. Sam didn't come to see me at all. My mind was in a turmoil. I had left them with all my property, my store, my home, my car, my jewelry, and money; they got everything. At least, I could get $50 or a $100 a month. Man, I wasn't gettin' nothin'. You could imagine how my mind was reelin'.

The first job I got at Leavenworth was in the kitchen, cleaning tables off. I made about $35 a month doing that job. With that money, I bought me three or four jars of peanut butter, a couple of cases of ramen noodles, something to eat on. Ya,' know that ramen noodles ain't nothing but starch. That was a regular meal. I survived off of that $35 a month in Leavenworth. My next job was buffing floors in A-Hall. My partner was out of Little Rock, Arkansas.

I ran into lots of good guys in my life who told me, don't worry about nothing, that I couldn't change and that I couldn't control things, cause worrying ain't going to do nothing but kill 'ya. So, I'm listening to what they said and they took me by my hand and said, well, if you gonna be here, you might as well make some good out of it. Go ahead and get ya education. So I went back to school in 1979. They started me off 'bout second grade and come all the way back up with my English, math, and reading comprehension. I was a little embarrassed, but they kept telling me, don't worry bout that, you know it's better late than never. You be a fool to be up in here and don't take advantage of getting an education when they giving it away free. So I went in there and started. I stayed in there going on four years. I was in AA, chemical abuse classes, anger management classes, trans-psycho analysis and rational analysis classes. In Rational Analysis, we just sat around in groups and talked about life, you know. Asking each other, you know, if you was in that situation again, knowing what you know now, how would you deal with that? So we lifted each other up and let 'em know you going to be back locked down because that's what got you here before. So we got a chance to let other people see us and how we think and felt. Saying nah, that's wrong man, don't do it like that. I had a chance to go to group therapy with these cats and once I got involved, that really helped me, you know. Lots of these cats were X people that had been in trouble for doing this and doing that.

Quite naturally when you in jail, you get strong mentally, physically, and spiritually because you don't have many devices that you can get into, like alcohol and drugs. Don't get me wrong, there is a little drugs up there. But man, them people got that Penitentiary tight as Dick's Hat Band. There ain't no drugs up in there now. In the old days might have been a lot of it. But in these days, no, Lordy! It teaches you, no, forces you, to think rationally, you know. It teaches you to use your time wisely because you ain't got no choice. Either learn something from this experience and show that you've learned something when you walk up out of here.

But you don't know if you going to make it through this time. Leavenworth is a dangerous penitentiary. I saw a lot of stuff go down in there. Man! A lot of stuff. Lots of stabbings, killings, and assaults. You be fallin' out the way, like somebody be tryin' to get you. You just be trying to get the hell out the way, you know. Cause them knives ain't got no eyes. It's scary as hell!

I stayed at Leavenworth going on five years. My security status dropped and in 1984 they sent me down in Memphis, Tennessee. I was at FCI. When I went down there, things changed. At Leavenworth, they kept us locked up. Every night before four-'o-clock count, everybody was locked up. You didn't even get a chance to see outside no more. When the stars came out, you didn't get a chance to see them no more. You know, I didn't realize how important being able to walk around outside when you got ready was. Being able to see and enjoy stuff. They had count three times a day at Leavenworth. In the morning at 7:00; they count again at 4:00 P.M. They count again at 10:00 P.M. Most of the time you were on lockdown.

At Memphis we didn't have to go in in the evenin'. We could stay out in the yard, all the way up to 8 o'clock in the evening. When I first got there, I would sit on the Yard, checkin' out the stars and moon, smokin' some reefer, and drinkin' some home hooch. Man! It seemed like I was damn near home. Seemed like I was almost on the street. The only thing that was missing now, was some soul food and some sex. That hooch and weed was good at that time. But ain't nothin' like your freedom!

I stayed down at FCI 'til about 1988; went back and forth to the Parole Board and they kept denying me. So that made nineteen years on that seventeen-year bit. That was from 1979 to 1989. I got out and caught another case. You can imagine how I felt. I had been home twenty-three months. Man! I had opened my store back up, and got it ready; fixed up my apartment buildings on Thekla and Penrose, and in the 6600 block of Sacramento. I had put all my buildings back together. I was rollin' on top. I look around, I done got popped on a bunch of bullshit. They gave me another 17 years for being on a gun range. They went back and used my prior convictions. Something I already served time for. They gave me more time the second time, more than they did the first time. That should have been a violation of the double jeopardy law. The double jeopardy law says no one can be convicted twice for the same crime; nor can they use that conviction to go with another case, to give me more time for that case. They turned a blind side to the double jeopardy law, with some legal bullshit. They were now classifying me as a career offender. How can they give a man all that time for a gun and it wasn't a crime of violence? The question is, does the career offender law apply to legal actions involving the same offense? But this is what they do. It don't matter if you been tried, sentenced and served time on charges. The gun was not connected with any violent crime. The career offender statute does not apply in this situation. But the system let them get away with it. They can make the law then turn right around and break that law.

So I went through all of that. I went to Algoa where I stayed another year. That made eleven years after I got out in '89. I came right back in '90. I stayed down four years and seven months—more than I did the first time. You don't think that wasn't enough to make somebody go crazy? I just kept sayin' to myself, "Keep your will to live' cause it was almost like being dead! You know. And I knew that I had done this to myself. So I just didn't wanna' lay down and die. I had made the choices so I said "Uh, I'm going to keep on trying to get back out there. So do what you gotta' do."

I was reading, writing, going to school, exercising, Bible study, fellowshipping, following God's basic instructions, and being in control of my temper and everything else. Whatever it was going to take, I could not fail. I made it!

The first bit I got in one fight in 10 years, you know. My second bit I went to the Hole, one time for a dirty urine in 15 years, that's all; no fights, none of that. No insubordination, none of that. Wasn't caught with no weapon, none of that. I was determined, to have control of myself, my choices, and actions. I wanted to be in control to the point to where I would never be making bad choices regarding my freedom or trying to hurt someone and end up locked down again. So I learned from them bad choices how to make better choices.

It's time to talk about Mama. Her name was Naomi. Her maiden name was Naomi Lane. Her married name was Murphy. My mother was born in Blytheville, Arkansas. She use to sit me down and tell me the story of how she came up in Blytheville. She and her twin sister were the only children born to her mother and father. Her twin passed away at birth.

My mother said that her mother and father owned a farm in Blytheville. She told me they had lot of blacks that worked for them on their farm. She would go around in Blytheville and recruit workers who did not have jobs to work on her parents' farm. Some of these blacks did not have food to eat, and/or were homeless.

During the summer time when it was time to serve lunch, she would ring this big ol' bell that she held in her hand. Everyone would come in from the field and eat. Then they would go back to work. In the evening time when work was done, she would ring the bell and everyone would come in from the field.

My mother told me when she had her farm that a white man tried to steal a cow off her farm and she shot and killed him. She was sentenced to five years in prison and she was working in the warden's office. Her job was to clean his office and feed the prisoners that were in the Hole.

She said that they kept the black prisoners locked down with iron balls and chains around their ankles and that they had been in the Hole so long that the iron cuffs on their ankles was causing serious infections to their ankles, causing them to rot and smell. She said black prisoners were treated inhumanely, not even given medical treatment for their injuries. She also said that when she took food down to the Hole, she would take some turpentine, sticking the turpentine up between her legs to hide it. She would treat the inmates' sores that were caused by the iron cuffs. She said the turpentine would kill the maggots and heal the wounds. She said if they had caught her doing that, they would have killed her, but she took the risk.

Mama said after she finished doing her time in Blytheville, they ran her out of Blytheville and told her she could never come back there again. Mama left and came up here to St. Louis. At that time, she did not have any children.

One day after she had all three of us, she told me that she had still owned the farm in Blytheville. She said she slipped back down there and sold the farm to a preacher and later on, the preacher was supposed to have sold the property to the Highway Patrol.

Mama use to tell me how they did not want her back in that city. She said she never wanted her children to be born and raised in the South. That's why she migrated and came North. She eventually became involved in politics. She was a Easter

Star. She too, was always active in the community, organizing and feeding the homeless who didn't have anything. She was always active in politics. Telling people how to vote, who to and not to vote for. Mama held down Leffingwell and Cass as Precinct Captain. She was always encouraging people to vote. My brother Sam was always at Mama's side. The polling place was on Leffingwell and Cass in a little shoe store; before that it was in a drug store. Our house was in the same block as the polling place; 1420 N. Leffingwell. She was active at the polling place for fourteen or fifteen years. My brother Sam stayed up under her, watching her. That's where he got a lot of his political awareness and knowledge from.

My mother was a civil rights fighter. She believed in change. She loved people and helpin' them. That was something in her nature that she could not help. white folks never liked Mama. But they had to respect her, because she had so much power with her people and politicians in the community.

My mind is going back on how to tell this story, of how Lorenzo and Sam came about. As I sat here in my bedroom; I just woke up. When tellin' about Sam I want to be able to shed light on the growing up of Sam Petty in the city of St. Louis. On how his mind was transformed from a poverty-stricken ghetto brother to a revolutionary at an early age. When I think back about my brother, I recall how strong minded and intelligent he was.

Sam was run over by a car when he was about six years old. The accident took place on Leffingwell and Cass. He was running out of an alley when the car hit him. The car drug him almost to the corner, with Sam stuck under the front end. I couldn't have been no more than five, but I remember Sam had just started in the kindergarten. I was about ready to start.

Sam had just left the store and had hid a bag of candy upstairs in the house then went back downstairs. I heard somebody holler, "Sam just got hit by a car!" I was upstairs looking for the candy, you understand. Mama broke down the stairs yelling "Lord! Oh Lord! My baby!'

I thought, wait a minute, man, this sounds like something

serious. So I stopped searching for the candy and ran from the second floor. Then I saw a crowd of people. I saw my daddy —he was running up and down the street with a knife in his hand, shouting "Where's the guy at? Where's the guy at? I'm going to kill the guy! I'm goin' to kill the son of a bitch!"

The car was on top of Sam. Mama was saying "Oh Lord! Somebody, help me. Oh Lord! Somebody help my baby." The ground was so hot. A man took off his shirt and put it under Sam's head and back. The street was burnin'. Mama bent down and put her back to the car. She said, 'Oh Lord! Have mercy!" She picked the car up off of Sam and said, "Get my baby." Some people drug him out from under the wheel.

Sam stayed in Homer G. for a whole year in a body cast from his neck all the way down to his ankles; he was busted up. They wired him up with cat wire. They said he would not be able to walk again.

Sam was out of school for almost a year. There was some wine-heads from the corner, Mr. Elliot, and Mr. Jones, who would always work with Sam on his education. He was out of school again for almost a year, rehabilitating. But during that time, Mr. Elliot and them were teaching Sam. When he did go back to school, the only thing I remember was him getting doubles.

Sam was never the type of person that like for nobody to put their hands on him, because he had been busted up so bad. He came home from Boonville in 1964. He had been there for killing Bow. He had been there for a couple of years. When he got out, they were rioting around Leffingwell and Cass. Sam was sixteen, I was fifteen, and Joe was fifteen. We were unaware of it, but our lives were at a turning point, they tumblin'. We were youngsters and askin', "what the hell is this?"

During the rioting they broke Sam's arm, they broke Joe's leg, and busted my head and face up. They didn't think nothing about Sam Petty having been broken and busted up, when he was hit by that car. They also didn't know how they affected our minds, especially Sam's.

They sent us all back to jail. They sent Sam back to Boonville. When they did that to Sam, his mind flipped; he began making a transformation. He became a Muslim. He started walking around with the Muhammad Speaks newspaper. Eventually he started the Black Liberators. I looked around again, he and some other brothers were havin' meetings damn near every night in the Central West End. He then took the movement on the road. He started protesting with H. Rap Brown and other black revolutionary families. They started going from city to city, protesting against injustices against blacks. They also were protesting for equal rights in employment and housing. That's what they were fighting for.

The Man made it look like Sam was a criminal. Made it like he was trying to take over something. The only thing that Sam Petty and Rap Brown were trying to do was wake black people up to all the injustices that blacks were suffering, and the lack of equal opportunities. They wanted equal rights in education, housing, and employment; we were not getting any of that. They were rolling across the country with what they called and Underground Revolutionary Movement. This movement had been put together by the Black Panthers, Black Stone Rangers, and other revolutionary-minded brothers. Sam and Rap helped organize all the brothers all up in Chicago, all over the world. They went around the world protesting.

They had to stay on the move. The white Man knew what they were doing. When they caught with Sam and Rap, they were in New York City. That's when Sam ended up in prison.

Sam Petty had been brutalized by police as a young black man coming up, from fifteen on up, from Boonville on up, to Danamora Penitentiary in New York.

While Sam was in the hospital in a body cast, he told me that they gave him one hundred pain shots a day. I couldn't imagine that; tears fell from my eyes. This was my brother, Sam Petty, the revolutionary. He was responsible for starting and organizing the Black Liberators Organization at 2810 Franklin. They had a big mural on a wall, on Leffingwell and Franklin. The mural was called the Wall of Respect. The mural had the pictures of all the black leaders on it; some leaders that some

56

black people had never heard of. The Black Liberators were educating us. They even had a black newspaper out called the Black Liberator. The Black Liberators were a group of brothers who were dedicated to the cause and were ready to fight and give their lives, in order to improve and uplift humanity. That was my big brother Sam.

I need to clear up something about my brother Sam and Rap Brown when they was up there in New York in '70 and '71. That's when they were set up and sent to prison on some bullshit charges. There was a shoot-out, coming up out of the Red Carpet Bar in Manhattan in '71.

I got out of the state penitentiary from Behind the Wall on May 10, 1972. My brother Joe picked me up, we discussed a lot of things that had been going on, he updated me. He started telling me about Sam and Rap and their situation in New York. I asked him what the purpose was. And Joe told me that Sam and Rap didn't like the way drug dealers was operating when it came to them kids, They had them young- sters selling heroin on the streets to other youngsters who were beginning to O. D. real heavy. Frank Lucas and 'em was putting it out there so pure that the youngsters didn't know how to cut it.

Sam and Rap decided to do something about it. Joe told me that he recruited nine people from St. Louis and took them to New York City. When they got there, Sam told him they had inside information on the dudes connected with all the drug dealers who were sitting on big money and buildings that the drug dealers owned. Joe said Sam and Rap started takin' over. They started takin' them niggers' buildings, taking money from 'em, and started taking they drugs from 'em. Joe was telling me that Sam and 'em was flushing the drugs down the toilet and was collecting money off them buildings.

Joe say one night they went into the Red Carpet Bar in Manhattan. That's when somebody hit the robbery button. Joe said there were five of them: Rap, Sam, Levi, Tank Slim, and him. He says after they got inside and then looked back outside, there were police everywhere; all of them heavily armed. Joe says a shoot-out followed. They were exchanging fire with the police from inside the bar.

They knew it wasn't going to last long because of a lack of ammo. Joe says they decided to lay down fire for each other, while each one broke up, out the bar. Joe told me the first one to run up out of there was Rap. He made it out of there but got shot in the stomach, while running across the street, to a building; then Tank Slim broke into the building across the street. Next, Sam broke, next was Levi. Joe said he laid down fire for him. Joe also said in the process of him holding fire for Levi, the police shot him in his right hip. That shot knocked him on his booty. Joe says he jumped back up, threw the pistols under a car, and got lost in the New York crowd that had gathered.

Joe says that while he was in the crowd, the man went up in the building they all ran into and brought Rap out on a stretcher, along with Sam, Levi, and Tank Slim. Joe says while he was in the crowd, he heard Sam asking, "Where's my brother?" "Where's my brother?" You know he was worried about Joe. He thought maybe that since he hadn't seen him, he might have got shot and gone down. Joe says he kept moving with the crowd. He then caught a bus with the bullet in his hip. He says he rode the bus to his friend's house.

Later on Sam told me that when the police came into the building to arrest them, the first policeman that came through the door threw a pistol in his face and just kept pulling the trigger. The pistol just kept clicking and clicking and clicking. Sam said once the police realized that he was out of bullets, he slapped him side the head with the gun and when he fell to the ground, he began kicking him.

That's the story of the encounter between Sam and H. Rap Brown and the man in New York. For those who don't, but want to, know about the New York City conflict, I have this to say. Sam and Rap were top-shelf brothers. Everything they were connected with was huge in scope, and operation. It is insulting to brand them as petty robbers.

I need to share something about a brother that answered the call. I want to pay tribute to Leon Dent, one of the original brothers in the Black Liberators Organization. I also want to reveal how he died Behind the Wall in Jefferson City, Missouri. At that time, the penitentiary was under the watch of Donald Warwick.

I had just been released from prison, on May 10, 1972. I and my brother Joe went back up Behind the Wall in the seventies on a baseball team. While Behind the Wall we got a chance to see brother Dent.

As we were leaving from Behind the Wall, Leon followed the truck we were on; holding on to the tailgate. We were sitting on the end of the truck, he was running behind the truck and wouldn't let go. The only thing he was saying was "Ah! My man", all the time we were going up the hill. I kept telling him that everything is going to be alright, my man.

After we left, I think it was no more than a couple of years after that Leon got into a confrontation with some Kansas City boys. He had a fight with about fifteen of them. They tell me he whipped all 'em ass and took they knives from 'em, and everything.

Donald Warwick, the warden, hated Leon because Leon was a Revolutionary Brother. Leon did not like to see nobody messing over nobody. He especially didn't like to see men taking advantage of them young boys, turning them into homosexuals; he really didn't like that. And that's what was going on back there, then. Them guys was tryin' to turn them young guys out.

Leon kept getting involved and kept whipping they ass about messing with them boys. Warwick put Leon in the Hole, he says for Leon's protection. Now, I don't understand why come Warwick didn't just transfer him if he was worrying about Leon's safety. He left Leon in the Hole.

Back in the Sixties when Leon was protesting with Reverend Charles Koen and the Black Liberators, Ninth District Police beat up Leon and Reverend Koen. They busted Reverend Koen's arms and head. They did Leon the same way. But after that incident of police brutality, Leon started having seizures caused by the police beatings.

Leon had a seizure one day while in the Hole, up under B-Hall. The Guards came around and saw him in his cell. They called Warwick and told him about Leon's condition. Warwick had them put a sheet around his neck and hung him up in the cell door bars, as if he committed suicide.

Well, I went to Leon's funeral. I also paid for Leon's funeral an autopsy. His funeral was at Ted Foster's up on Grand. I went to the burial and everything. The results of the autopsy confirmed that Leon did not die from a seizure. Leon died from strangulation caused by the sheet tied around his neck. Nothing was ever done about it. That's the story of how the Revolutionary Brother, Leon Dent, went out. Everyone in the know knew that the Boss had them racist guards lynch Brother Dent.

I want to talk about Forest City, Arkansas, and when I was coming home in 2007. Right before the time when I was getting ready to come home after fifteen years of confinement. I had one year left when they put me in the Hole. It all came about because of a confrontation between the blacks and the Mexicans, over a T.V. The administration had given the blacks an extra T. V. The Mexicans wanted to take over this T. V. They felt that since they had the manpower, they could pull it off—that's when the conflict came about. The blacks told the Mexicans, naugh, you can't take this T. V., over our dead bodies.

It wasn't no more than five or six of us that stood up against about twenty or thirty Mexicans. Other blacks cowered down, saying, "Man, I ain't got nothing to do with it.‘ The five or six of us said, "We came here as men, y'all ain't going to do us like this. One of the Mexicans went to a locker and got a belt, wanting to hit the brother that made the statement. The brother told the Mexican, "Put down that belt and I'll beat your ass'. He didn't put down the belt and they didn't take the T. V.

The next day the blacks recruited about three or four more blacks; that made nine or ten of us. One of the counselors in there told us, "Man, whatever you do, don't let them Mexicans run over you, do what you got to do." Well, we stood our ground.

Since they had me down as the leader, creating, organizing,

and keeping things going, they got this Mexican Police broad that was bringing in drugs to some Mexican prisoners, to put a joint in my locker. She came in one day when they was having a shakedown. I was in the T. V. room.

They called me out of the T. V. room. "Come here Petty, look what we just found in your locker." I said, "Man, you crazy'n than anyone. What I look like, putting a joint in my stupid locker, and I ain't got but a year left. And I ain't been in the Hole since I been here." I said, "You got me messed up man." And everybody, all the inmates said, "That's bullshit, somebody framed Lo."

So, they put me in the Hole. My counselor heard about it and he knew it was bullshit. So the next day when he came to work he tells me, she walked up to him and said, "Sorry I had to get your boy." He replied, "Bitch! Before it's over with they gone to be walking you up out of here in handcuffs." Well, 'sho nuff, they did. It took 'em six months to catch her. When they did catch her, the same counselor ran her down. She tried to throw the dope away, but they got her. They even busted the dude she been bringing it into. He snitched her out. He was the mule that was picking it up. He then ran it to the rest of them. Well, he wasn't about to take no case. So he told who were the people involved, where he was picking it up and who were the people he was taking it to, and when she was gone to bring it in, the next time. That's when they busted her.

I stayed in the Hole for six months on solitary confinement. I was locked down twenty-three hours a day. The penitentiary was so crowded, even the Hole was filled. The cells in the Hole were designed for two inmates. But now there were three inmates to each cell, and only two bunks. One inmate had to sleep on the floor. There was one toilet in each cell. When one inmate took a shit, the other two had to smell it as well. When one farted, the other two had to smell that.

So I did six months in solitary confinement, locked down twenty-three hours a day. Every morning I would do Bible study in my cell; never missed. and the inmates in the cell always studied with me, since I was doing it at a certain time.

I was in five or six different cells while I was in the Hole, with different inmates. I found out later that they were constantly putting inmates in the cell where I was, when one got moved out. I asked the lieutenant in the Hole, "why were you always putting somebody in the cell where I was, as soon as and inmate left." He whispered to me, "I'm not picking on you, but it's something about you that I can't put my finger on. But every inmate that had been in a cell with you came out a different person." He said, "I don't know what you sayin' to 'em, but it's working." He also said, "I'm a preacher on the streets. Whatever it is, when they leave your presence, they be a new man." God used me in the Hole like that; He gave me lessons.

While I was in the Hole, this Mexican inmate came to me for help. He wanted me to write a letter to his kids on what and what not to do in them streets. He didn't have any street knowledge on raising children and what to tell them what to avoid and what they should be doin' to stay out of trouble. How to be careful, and what to look forward to. I sit down and wrote this twelve- or fifteen-page letter for him, to his sons. All through prison, God was usin' me to minister and give people my knowledge to guide them through prison.

The System stuck it to me again a couple of weeks after I got out the Hole. I was released to the streets and halfway house and had been in the halfway house for six months. That's when they snatched me off the streets, locked me down in the Jennings Police Station for 'dirty urine'. I had a bad back, with arthritis in my back, hands, and knees. My wife had the same thing, so I took some her medicine. I didn't have no money, I had nothin'. So I came up with the 'dirty urine' and was locked down for takin' barbiturates. I was locked down in Jennings for two months. Man! When I got out of the Jennings Police Station and put my feet on the ground outside on Jennings Station Road, it was like my equilibrium was off; I was wobbly. I could hardly stand up. They had kept me locked in that cell with no movement goin' on two months. By the grace of God, I made it out of there. I was diabetic and had high blood pressure. They had done so many things tryin' to kill me even when I came home.

Even after I came home, I was going to see my parole officer every month for three and a half years. He even came to my house every month just to drop in on me. But he did not find anything because I wasn't doin' nothinjSo they eventually stop harassin' me. But that's what I went through in comin' home.

Now I live to be a free man. I'm not on parole, ain't on no bond, and I don't serve the Devil any more. Many temptations have arisen since I came home in 2007. I've had many 'ol so-called associates that was, and still are, sellin' heroin, cocaine, pills, and everything. Saying, "Hey baby, I got this, if you want it, let me know." I've been there, done that! I call it C&C: Choices and Consequences. I don't make them kind of choices no more. I advise every man, go to work. Cause if you ain't got no forty points built up in your Social Security, you can't draw a full Social Security check; go to work. Thirty-five points, thirty-two points ain't going to get it at sixty-two. You going to need those forty points to draw a full Social Security Check at 65 or 66. So you got to go to work and earn forty points.

The dope game ain't goin' to last forever. You can't make no career on doin' wrong. Only a fool keeps thinking he can keep doin' wrong, because he ain't never been caught. You can get away a thousand times over a period of time. But once they catch you for that one thing, partner, they gone to make you do enough time for everything you got away with. Ain't nothin' in the world worth sacrificing your life and freedom for, unless you are tryin' to protect your life.

Today is December 6, 2017. I wanna' talk about when I came home from Forest City, Arkansas. I was released from there after serving fifteen years and seven months. I had served most of my sentence. Once I had did my time, I was released to the streets. I had so many hours to get back to St. Louis. I had so many hours to get in the halfway house. It was a joy that I had been waitin' for, since I was forty-two years old, when I went in. When I got out, I was fifty-seven. So you can imagine how I felt.

A female friend picked me up and brought me back to St.

Louis and dropped me off at the halfway house; I then checked in. I was assigned a caseworker. Caseworkers are supposed to prepare you for the streets, assist with your living arrangements and finding a job. They didn't give me no bus fare, and no money to get around to find no job. They just release you from prison. They give you four hours to find a job. Now can you imagine, you got four hours to be in the streets, ridin' around from point A to point Z, lookin' for a job. I rode around with some help from some people. I didn't know where to go. I didn't know what to do, I was lost.

My cousin started comin' by to pick me up and takin' me around. I had to give him a few dollars to put in his tank. That went on for a couple of weeks. Then a friend of mine he kicked in and started picking me up, and droppin' me of at different places. After that, I had another female friend with a Bronco, pickin' me up and helpin' me. This turned out to be a great help to me. Then someone told me, he says go up to AARP. This was a job site for people 55 on up. I went over there and got hired at the Goodwill at 1726 Locust. I went down to the Goodwill working for a lady named Ms. Lillian. My job was janitorial work, changin' trash can liners, sweepin' and moppin' floors, cleanin' toilets, and dusting. I worked down at Goodwill, I say about eleven months. But then I got transferred to a job at St. James Catholic Center. My job there was janitorial and I did well there. I worked there for a couple of years. But then I got hired to work at another janitorial site. I use to go out to Brentwood, cleanin' up the Best Buy store. I worked out there, doing that job for about eleven months or a year. After I left there I got hired down at a place down on Broadway doing janitorial work. I worked down there for about a year.

My right knee was givin' me a lots of problems during that time. While I was working at Proctor & Gamble, my right knee locked up on me. Well, I had to go to the hospital and have a knee replacement. After that, I got hired back at St. James Catholic Center. At that time my wife was paying the notes on a 2007 Nissan Maxima. It became too much for her financially and she let it go. Up until that point that was my transportation. After that I went on and got me a Buick to ride around in. I was now able to get around much better. But my support wasn't there because I didn't have enough family. I moved out in Hazelwood with my family, which was my wife. She was too busy tryin' to take care of the grandkids and not me. So I left and came back to the house at 6600 Sacramento. The house was paid for. I didn't have anything turned on but the electric. The only heat I had on was the space heaters in my bedroom, the toilet, and one in the basement for the pipes. When I got up in the morning, I turned on the oven in the kitchen and that would warm the entire house up, so I stayed warm.

I cleaned and fixed my house up. It was clogged up with everything. They left junk in the hallway and basement. The house was full of junk. They had torn it up! I got it all together while I was there.

One day the Social Security people called me. They told me I was qualified for a disability check which was close to five hundred and somethin' dollars. I was now able to make it off that. But I didn't get it until I was out here almost three years. Up until that point I use to go every month to three or four food pantries and get them can goods, and all the food they had to give me. Every place that I knew that was givin' some assistance, passin' out food and clothes, I would go. I stocked up on can goods and the food that I received from the food pantries; that's how I made it. And then Social Security started givin' me Food Stamps. I was blessed; I was gettin' around two hundred dollars; that was a great feelin'.

But somewhere down the line the bastards cut me off from that. They cut me all the way down to around forty or fifty dollars. But I continued to hit the food pantries. I even went down to Reverend Rice on several occasions with Don Quan, better known as The Man, He showed me how to go in there and get that food from Reverend Rice. Every time I went lookin' I got me some needed food and clothing, nice stuff. I then found out about this Goodwill place over there on Forest Park. They sell a lot of used clothing and fixtures. I started goin' over there and I found lots of good clothes and shoes.

I had several places that I use to go to but those were the main ones. I had no place else to go.

On holidays like Thanksgiving and Christmas, I made it my business to find places that were passin' out stuff. Luther Boykins was one of 'em. Every year he was passin' out turkeys. So I made it my business to get me a couple of them. I never missed nothin' on holidays in the City, when they was givin' stuff out that I needed. I couldn't afford to miss 'em.

I couldn't have kept my focus and stayed on top of my business had I not continued to do Bible study the whole time I was in the penitentiary. I promised God if he protected me, guided me, and made a way for me, when I got out of there I wasn't gone to do wrong no more. Now! I promised God that. They say be careful what you promise God and be careful what you ask him for, so I stuck with that. Before I had depended on my colleagues and sellin' illegal narcotics to make my money. This was the first time that I came home from the penitentiary and didn't sell no dope. I stuck with my plan. I kept workin' jobs and kept goin' to the food pantries and when I started getting them Social Security disability checks that really helped me. There was Food Stamps but later on down the road they cut them. Later they cut my Social Security down to about forty-five dollars. A couple of years later they increased it again, to around ninety-six dollars.

When I turned sixty-two, I started receiving a Social Security check. Now I was receiving a Disability check, Social Security and Food Stamps, which were later disallowed. I can take care of myself now. I'm still living off my Social Security, Disability and food packages. I found me a church to go to, Sunny Mount on West Florissant. When I go there on Sundays I say to the world I couldn't have made it without my faith in God, stayin' focused and prayer. Now I have tapped into resources like the Weatherization Program. They helped me out with my house, as did Rebuilding Together, St. Louis and through all of them I was able to get my house fixed up without any money. It wasn't nothin' but "God's blessings." I say to you from experience when I was focused on doing what the Devil wanted me to do, it lasted a minute and I was back in jail. This was the first time I came home from prison that I stayed focused on what God wanted me to do and since that time, I haven't had anything but blessings come my way. So my support system was that I was able to walk my Faith, I thank God every day, all day, for his blessings all this time. Because ain't nobody gone to do what God can do for you and what you can do for yourself. Stay away from crime 'cause it don't pay. If you want to stay out here and enjoy life, get you a job, and stay away from everybody that's doin' wrong!

Now I wanna' talk about the Rules of the Street. My Rules of the Street came from my mother and father as I was growing up. My mother always told me what she thought was right and wrong; so did my father. Back then, I didn't have nobody else to listen to. I didn't have nobody else to tell me what was right or wrong but my mother and father—that's where your rules start at about life and the streets.

My mama always told me if somebody wasn't bothering you, leave 'em alone. But she always told us if somebody was bothering you and decide to jump on you, she always told us to fight back and don't come home cryin'. Because if we did, she was goin' to give us the ass whipping and the beat down that the streets wasn't ever gonna give us. She also told us two wrongs can't make no right.

My mother never told me to go out and rob nobody. She never told me to go out and shoot nobody. I was hangin' in the street because I wasn't going to school. I learned hustlin' and stealing from the streets. When we went hustlin' back in the day, we didn't carry no gun; for what? If you did somethin', when the police caught you, you went to jail.

Now, when it came to the narcotic world, people always was sayin' if you sellin' dope and somebody stick up your man or you with a gun, you got to go and retaliate the same way they brought it to you; well, I understand that. If you call the police on somebody in the narcotics game because you got stuck up, those in the game call that bein' a punk, they call that bein' a snitcher. Nobody wanted to be called a punk or a snitch 'cause somebody robbed you, a dope dealer, and you couldn't handle it on your own. But I'm here to say, there's a reason for everything.

Didn't nobody tell me back then what I know now; if I had knew then what I know now and somebody stuck up one of my dope dealers, I would have analyzed the situation. Say, look man, you out there, sellin' dope, you got to be alert at all times, you can't be sleeping. You got to be watching over your shoulder for everybody. You got to keep that thang in your hand; you should know that. If one of your people put his self in a situation where he let somebody rob him, he the one that got to handle that. Ain't no sense in you putting yourself on front street. If he ain't strong enough not to let somebody take something from him and go take care of his own business, he is to blame. No man should have to fight another man's battle. I never had nobody to stick up my dope dealers. If they had, I wouldn't have gone lookin' for 'em. Why would I risk my freedom, for five or fifteen hundred dollars that they took off my dope dealer, when he put his self in that situation. I was makin' too much money to go lookin' for somebody for five or fifteen hundred dollars and I grossing thirty thousand a week; that's peanuts. You got to analyze the situation when you in the game. You got to think big.

When you in the game they gone tell you, "Man, go for it!" They ain't say, "Hey! Don't do that; yeah, go ahead." They goin' to supe you up. 'Cause if you do something stupid and you get busted and or killed, they ain't got to worry about you no more you ain't got to worry 'bout yourself no more; if you ever do something like that and your ass end up locked down. You be sittin' up in there sayin' to yourself, "If I had a second chance to do it all over again. Man! I would have let that shit go. If I had walked past it and chalked it up as a loss. I still be out here, gettin' money."

When we were coming up and started pulling that trigger in the Narco-Game,when somebody robbed you or one of your people and you started shootin' that pistol, police were gone to jump all over you. What you need to understand is that it takes two to tango. You was out there and if you or your people had been alert and on their job it could never had happened. Everything happens for a reason. Most of the time it be a wake-up call. We just can't read the hand writin' on the wall. If you want to a success in life, you can't start squeezin' that trigger. You got to be man enough to think rationally enough to let that trigger play, lay quiet.

It's easy to get in trouble but it's a bitch gettin' out. It's easy gettin' into the penitentiary, but it's really hard gettin' out and once you get in there for squeezin' that trigger trying to impress a friend or an associate or family member, you realize that, hey man, if I had a chance to do it over again it would be different. Why? Because while you locked down after squeezin' that trigger, things change. You get on the phone and call home. Your family member tell you about your home-boy that you was runnin' with out there that you thought was your partner; he over there with your woman, and the first thing you think "what part of the game is that?'

If he had all that respect for you pullin' that trigger they wouldn't be over there, with your woman. If they had all that respect for you pullin' that trigger, they be sendin' you some money while you locked down. You would be able to go to the commissary and live the way you suppose to when you locked down.

But when you pull that trigger unnecessarily, that's when you learn that it just don't pay. There's a lot of things you ain't gonna know while you on the streets, about life. But when you go to the penitentiary after pulling that trigger, the first thing that comes to mind, well, if I knew that, I would have done it differently.

In the streets worryin' about what somebody say or what your home-boy gone say, is bullshit. They got a word, suped up! The person that suped, you up to do that. The regulars say let it go; he ain't your friend. He got somethin' else planned for you. He got plans to take over your business once you trip and make a mistake. He got plans of goin' by there, takin' your wardrobe, your car, and your woman; you just ain't been payin' attention. So what I suggest to all you young brothers out there, before you pull that trigger, always remember, there's certain things you can't take back. You can't take back what you say with your mouth. You can't call that bullet back once you pull that trigger. And you definitely can't bring a person's body back once you have killed them. So be careful about what you say, be careful about pullin' that trigger. By all means, every black man in America, listen to what I'm tryin' to share with you, all what nobody shared with me.

I messed up many a times in my life by thinking with my pride and feelings. I wish I had someone as wise and mature as I am now back then, to tell me what I'm sharin'with you all today. A slow dollar is a sho dollar. If you work hard, it might take longer, but it's guaranteed that you are going to be able to keep it and enjoy it. That's unless the Grim Reaper calls your number. It ain't guaranteed when you go out there and do something wrong that you gone continue to have and keep what you have accomplished. What does a man conquer when he gains the world, but loses his freedom? Once you lose your freedom, you might not get a second chance at getting up, out of the pen. And if you do, you are truly blessed. I'm saying that to every black man in America. Don't think with your pride; don't think with your feelings, think with a rational mind. Think about your freedom, think about being there for your sons and daughters and when they will need you. Think about your woman and your father. Ain't but one thing that will hurt you, and tear you down as when you have made irrational decisions and negative actions and you end up in the penitentiary. And your father dies and they won't let you go home to a damn funeral. What if your son ends up in the pen with you, for doing the same thing that got you there. Then you have to watch him get abused by the Administration, watch him get beat down and turned into a homosexual and there ain't nothin' you can do about it.

It don't pay to rob nobody, it don't pay to kill nobody about no money. You can always get more money. But it's hard getting out that pen. So think twice before you pull that trigger. If somebody makes you that mad, I would suggest to every black man in America, be man enough to walk away. I got and ol' saying now: It ain't about bein' a man, it's about bein' a better man. How do you be a better man? By walking away and following God's basic instructions before leaving earth. Only look for a trigger when it comes to protecting your property, your life, or a close family member. That's when you have no choice. Here's what you got to do to them. Use any force necessary. For the man who knows how to walk away and don't pull that trigger, the rewards are so great further down the road. One day you are going to be so glad that you walked away.

You can pull that trigger, but fifteen, twenty years from now, if they catch up to you, when you are on top of the world, and overnight they take everything that you accumulated, along with your freedom, you will understand where I'm comin' from.

The penitentiary is the closest thing to a graveyard as you get. When you die, you can't take nothin' with you, none of things you have accumulated. The penitentiary is the same way. Whatever you have accumulated out in the streets you cannot take to the penitentiary. You got to leave it all behind, like you never had it. Be a wise man, not a fool. Remember the Golden Rules. May God bless those who continue to follow these instructions.

There is no glory in doin' time. The people who you were trying to impress when you went to jail, and who you thought would be there for you, they won't. They won't come to visit you, write you, or send you any money. Many times I wished I'd stayed in school and listened to my parents. However I was locked into a life-style that I was unable to shake. The realities connected with incarceration are a grim afterthought of not being able to live a self-empowered, positive life. In prison you can't do anything that people normally do. In prison you can't do anything you want to. Everybody you thought you were cool with has disappeared, out of sight, and out of mind.

When you go to prison you find out that your worst enemy is your black brothers. I call this black-on-black crime. Then you have the white guards who harass you constantly. A large number of guards were racists, and found some kind of sick pleasure in the brutal way they treated black inmates. The inmates who were looking to make a reputation of being tough were a concern for the weaker inmates. And then there were the scam artists who loved to play games in order to get money out of you. Then you had those dangerous predators who were looking for young, weak, and confused inmates, to do their sexual bidding. Some inmates were homosexuals on the street. These inmates had incredible power. Some, too, were extremely dangerous. Homosexuals come in all sizes, from the not so large to the largest. Aside from the homosexual's lifestyle, they too, were masters of deceit. In all the prisons that I was in, homosexuals affected the operation of that institution from assaults, to murders.

In prison you find yourself working five days out of the week, and earning a monthly wage of only $15, sometimes only $5. When you were on the street, you didn't work at all. If you had worked like they make you work in prison, you would have never gone to prison. A fast dollar will put you in prison every time because you don't have the patience needed to earn that honest dollar. We can get the same things out of life if we work and take our time. It will take longer to get it but you will still be FREE and able to be with and enjoy your family. And do all the things you want to. Most of the time, we try to get what we want, but what we want all the time isn't what we need. Not putting their wants before their needs, they could be very successful in life. You can always accomplish more out of life if you work a job or work for yourself, than you could if you commit crimes. It is very important that you learn as a young man to channel your negative energy into somethin' positive. Positive actions will get you ahead in life and keep you on safe and solid ground. In that way you can enjoy the fruits of life. And you won't have to worry about gettin' caught lookin' over shoulder, going to prison, bein' killed, or havin' to suffer all those agonies that accompany livin' a negative existence.

Even if you are unlucky, poor, and have to do without, you

must be strong and see that staying positive is the best road to travel. When you channel your energy into negative thinking and actions, it will keep you on that one-way, dead-end road to failure, prison, or shorten your life here on earth. What is so disheartening about this condition, is that it is, and has been, a part of The Man's plan of racial genocide for black Americans, especially black men.

We need to channel our positive energies into education, and positive planning, so we can live a better life. That way you won't have to worry about goin' to prison or bein' killed. More importantly, you won't suffer the agony of a life being locked away like and animal, in a negative, dog-eat-dog environment, without happiness or success.

Getting into and committing crime is easy. Avoiding the consequences is extremely difficult. Penitentiary time is time wasted out of your life. There is a difference in the amount of time you will serve if you are convicted of state or federal crimes. Federal time is the longest. If you are convicted of a federal crime, you will serve eighty-five percent of your sentence before you are released. For instance, if you are given a ten-year sentence, you will serve eight years and about four months. On a fifteen-year sentence you will serve thirteen years and about four months.

When I went to prison I found myself reading all the time, to better myself, and better understand the law. I worked on,and got my G. E. D. You can also get a college education. If you had only done this when you were on the street, just imagine what you could have accomplished in life and made out of yourself. Many times, we were busy running the streets hustling, or trying to find some whore to lay up with. Hustling could even get you killed or land you in prison. Whores will beat you out your money and even get you killed if you get caught up in the wrong place.

You have to think all the time when you around criminals, and those who are up to no good. Being around negative people puts you in a no-win situation. Most negative people don't want anything good out of life. Therefore, they will try and keep you on their level because misery loves company. They will always have alcohol and drugs to feed you. These poisons make you do things that lead to negative results. Drugs and alcohol make you want to party all the time and before you know it, you are broke, and ready to go hustlin'. If your luck turns sour and you get caught, the good times turn ugly.

Depending on the circumstances, you could be facing penitentiary time. Sometimes you will lose your wife, children, and home. The cost of being locked down is the most devastating consequence you will pay for makin' negative decisions. Your children will grow up without you being there to share the experiences, the love, relationships, and fun. They will not have any positive memories of you. And if you were not cool with their mother, she might not have anything positive to say about you to your children. Doing time in prison without hearing from your family really hurts, and it takes something out of you. In other words, it robs you of your happiness. You have to be strong enough to motivate yourself to be happy every day. If you can't do that, you will not survive and make it out of the penitentiary. The quality of a man's character isn't measured by his good times, but how he handles his bad times. A man's bad times will break him down. Many people are not able to pull themselves together when they fall down. Until you have fallen down and had to pick yourself up, you will never know what you are made of. Those who can't make it go crazy or turn into alcoholics or drug addicts. They will end up without hope, or anything. You must be strong. One way of becoming stronger, is practicing every day to say "NO!" to those things that are negative, or it will bring you down. Saying NO! to things like usin' drugs, alcohol, and bein' disrespectful of people and their property. Being able to say NO! to drugs when so-called friends offer them to you. A friend will never mislead you, or do anything to bring you down. You must maintain a daily schedule of doin' things that will make you a better person, like reading and writing. Reading newspapers, and listenin' to news on the T. V. are good habits to develop. Also stay away from people who don't want anything out of life, and away from places where people are talking about or engaged in illegal actions; and are unemployed. Find a church to attend every Sunday and read somethin' from the Bible every day. When you stay focused on God's word, you stay strong and resist the Devil's temptations. Never let anyone make important choices for you. Ask people close to you for advice. Your parents, pastor, teacher, or relative will always tell you what you should do. You must stand for something positive or you may fall for something detrimental to your future or life. Never hook up with people from the streets who you think are your friends. Because you never know what's on their mind. They may rob and kill you. They may have a gun, or dope, or both on them, and leave them in your ride if the police pull you over. You more than likely will catch a case. Someone might be looking for them and start shooting at them, miss them and shoot you. Stay away from parties where you know there'll be lots of drinking and smoking weed. Many brothers can't hold their liquor and become hostile and start fighting with you, to show off in front of a woman who is not giving him any attention. Lots of women who don't have anything on the ball, love men who are always acting like they are a bad ass. A lot of dudes at parties who use drugs will rob you in order to get more drugs. These are people who do drugs all the time. Drug addicts are very dangerous, especially those who carry guns. Be very careful if you are dating a woman who lives in a bad neighborhood, and you go there to pick her up. Even if she lives in a good neighborhood, stay alert. Always take a woman to your place of choice, and not hers. She might run into one of her ol' boyfriends and want to show her ass. My sisters! Don't let a man take you to his house. Because sometimes if you refuse to have sex with him after he has spent money on you, he might take some sex. No one will hear you scream. Make sure you can trust him, and make sure he uses protection. Safe sex is always the wisest choice; better safe, than sorry. And ladies never go over to a man's house when he has lots of friends there. They could put somethin' in your drink that will knock you out. You then become easy prey, becomin' available for all of them to have their way with you. Women! Just because you are with another woman doesn't mean it can't happen. Sometimes your woman friend could be in on the plot. She won't let you know because some women do strange things for their man. Always keep a phone with you, in case of an emergency. Someone might try and bring harm to you. Keep a can of Mace with you; it may mean the difference between life and death. Everyone should be careful of where they park when they go out to shop or for entertainment. Park in a spot where you can see everything around you. Little boys and girls, never get in a car with a stranger when you are walkin' to or from school, or while you are out walkin'. No matter how desperate you may be, no matter how bad the weather or fast you need to be somewhere, keep walkin', you'll be safe. If the person or persons get out their vehicle, run like hell until you get to a safe place or see someone you know. Then have someone call the police. Remember as much as you can about the person and type of vehicle they were drivin'. Always be alert in your neighborhood, or any neighborhood, when gettin' in or out of your vehicle.

Young people, when your parents, teachers, pastor, or any adult tells you something that will benefit you, take it to heart, because it could get you ahead in life, or save your life. Please remember, crime does not pay. You should only hurt someone when they are trying to bring harm to you or your family. Always try to be comfortable with being by yourself because being dependent on others might lead to a downfall. Learn to love yourself and be at peace with yourself. Give your mind something to do by reading a good book or readin' your Bible. Bein' with the wrong people or in the wrong place could cause you a lot of trouble. Always remember, life's real riches are your faith in God, your freedom, your good health, a good job, and a good relationship with a woman. If you have these five things, you have more than any amount of money can ever give you. Remember if you take that short-cut in life to get your money, you will end up in prison or the graveyard. If you take the long road, you will always come out ahead of the game. It will take longer, but you will be FREE! And you will avoid all the agony that awaits you at the end of that one-way dead-end road. Young brothers, let this Manhood Guide lead you to your journey through life:

The Road to Manhood
Walking the Talk
Signs of Manhood:

1. A man respects himself and others.
2. A man keeps his word.
3. A man makes mistakes and admits them.
4. A man is strong enough to say, "I'm sorry."
5. A man studies and seeks knowledge.
6. A man respects the truth and lives by it.
7. A man respects his elders.
8. A man lives up to his responsibilities.
9. A man works.
10. A man believes in the creator.
11. A man leads and teaches by example.
12. A man supports his family.
13. A man defends those weaker than himself.
14. A man is strong enough to love.
15. A man is strong enough to forgive.
16. A man is affectionate with children.
17. A man is strong enough to tell the truth.
18. A man is strong enough to control himself.

Only you can enrich your manhood!!!

DEADLY - GANGSTA "1"

1. The Petty brothers, (L to R; Sam, Joe, Lorenzo). This is the only photo taken with all 3 adult Petty brothers taken together since their youth photos.
2. Seated L to R: Sam, Joe and Lorenzo Petty
3. Naomi Murphy holding her son Lorenzo Petty
4. Sam attending the funeral of his brother Joe. Also attending is H. Rap Brown (far right)
5. Joe Petty
6. Uncle Lorenzo Petty
7. Lorenzo Petty, Sr.
8. Sam Petty
9. Sam Petty holding his son Joe Petty

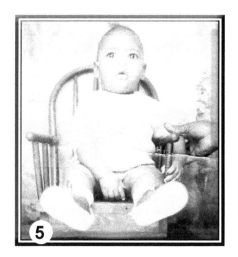

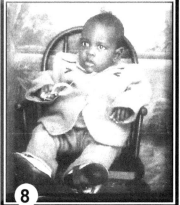

Printed in the USA
CPSIA information can be obtained
at www.ICGtesting.com
LVHW011914210823
755883LV00010B/341

9 781933 635484